Navigating Through The Valleys Of Success

Copyright © 2018

Navigating Through the Valleys of Success: A Perspective In Perseverance

Cleon Joseph

All rights reserved. No part of this publication may be reproduced, distributed, or transmitted in any form or by any means, including photocopying, recording, or other electronic or mechanical methods, without the prior written permission of the publisher, except in the case of brief quotations embodied in reviews and certain other non-commercial uses permitted by copyright law.

CJFF Publishing
15703 Condon Avenue C3
Lawndale, Ca. 90260
www.cjffpublishing.com

ISBN: 978-1-949856-02-6 (print), 978-1-949856-03-3 (epub)

Ordering Information:
Special discounts are available on quantity purchases by corporations, associations, and others. For details, contact
CJFF Publishing at the address above.

Scripture quotations from The Authorized (King James) Version. Rights in the Authorized Version in the United Kingdom are vested in the Crown. Reproduced by permission of the Crown's patentee, Cambridge University Press

Navigating Through The Valleys Of Success

A Perspective In Perseverance

Cleon Joseph

Contents

Foreword 1

Preface 3

The Seed Was Planted at the Top 5

Suppressing the Seed: The Ultimate Valley 9

Your Seed Will Be Forced Out of the Valley, Like It or Not 21

The Man of God Appears in the Valley of Despair 33

The Messenger of Assignment 39

An Angel's Message at Work 43

He Confirmed It In Spanish 47

He Kick-Boxed a Message 49

The Final Messenger in the Valley 51

When in the Valley, Move or God Will Move You! 57

Kaboom! We Have Arrived 69

The Valley of Implicitness: Good Credit Ain't Enough 75

Leave No Stone Unturned in the Valley 85

Pulling Out the Corporate Card in the Valley 91

You Have to Run Into a Few Idiots as You Climb 99

Surprise! I'm an MMA Coach? 105

You Cannot Help Everyone: Use Your Brain, Not Your Heart 109

First Taste of Prime Time as I Climb 113

The Circle of Relationships in the Valley 119

Reward for Your Effort in the Valley	135
Ego is One Hell of a Drug When Climbing	143
Be a Mentor, Not a Savior — Not Worth Your Marriage	147
Mentors Are Not Gods: At Some Point, Show Results	155
Secrecy Cannot Hold Excellence	159
A Vitamin B Shot Before Launch	165
Los Angeles, We Have Lift-Off	169
Branded in 60 Seconds . . . Credit a Python	179
The Fine Line Between Promotion, Giving, and Pain	185
From Cynical to Singing It from the Stage	191
A Chance to Make It Right	197
God's Plan	203
The Show Must Go On In the Valley	207
Maybe a Failure for Hollywood, Victory for God's Will	213
Tragedy Does Not Care About Your Passion Project	223
The Champ Goes Down, But Rises	231
When a Film Segment Turns Into a Eulogy	235
All Ready to Go, On the Shelf for Now	239
Don't Quit Your Day Job	245
A Joseph Returns from the Pit . . . a Boss	251
The Conclusion Is Not In This Book	253
Prologue	263
Special Thanks	267
About The Author	273

Foreword

We've all seen those well-manicured presentations from people who want to make an impression. Some wear their personas in person, some on social media, some from the stage and screen. But victories without struggle or in the absence of challenge, cause healthy skepticism and fail to command our attention. This is why there is an allure with cinematic features such as *Rocky, Rudy, Secretariat, Million Dollar Baby, Slumdog Millionaire, Cinderella, Cinderella Man* and *The Pursuit of Happyness*.

Perhaps the reason historical figures such as Martin Luther King Jr., Gandhi, Abraham Lincoln, Winston Churchill and Nelson Mandela inspire us, is because their victories came through days of toil, deficits, setbacks, misfortunes and trial. It is here we witness their humanity and discover a commonality that resonates with our own hope-filled dreams. We mere mortals find our own life stories inextricably entangled with theirs.

In life's valley experiences, the suffering soul, emotionally heavy and sometimes dark, needs soothing. Through a simple sense of the shared human struggle, we all find solace, and the courage to continue on.

Successes or "mountain top" experiences are often glorious, yet the details chronicled from our journeys prove invaluable. This is the essence of Cleon Joseph's accomplishment in the pages that follow. He takes the thoughtful reader down a path of discovery by first revealing his acquaintance with sorrow, which is in itself cathartic. Cleon does not, however, leave us in a valley of despair, but instead recounts his rise from the ashes of disheartenment.

The way he fearlessly bears his soul, revives our belief in the redemption of our own stories.

This work is one to be pondered thoughtfully, as its content emerged from tried wisdom rather than speculative theory. Whether you are perched high above life's valleys or currently find yourself in the center of one, this book is for you. If you are experiencing favorable outcomes or unusual despair, this life-giving work will help.

As long as we live on this terrestrial sphere called Earth, the cycle of treading atop peaks and traversing through gorges will persist. You though, now hold in your hand a potent tool to aid in navigating your way through life's many valleys. Let Cleon guide you through.

Preface

By Eva Joseph

Cleon Joseph has been my best friend for almost thirty years and as of November 2017, we have been married for twenty years. I met him when he was seventeen years old, at California State University of Long Beach. I have been by his side, through the good and the challenging times, as he navigated many valleys of success as a son, father, brother, friend, employee, businessman, and most importantly to me, as my husband. Just like all people mastering success, we've gone through struggles, challenges and triumphs that groomed us for the next level of growth.

In this book, Cleon reveals his journey through valleys, to inspire you not to quit on your dreams. He recollects memories with vivid details, so you can clearly paint the pictures in your mind, merging your journey in step with his. He shares how the fear of success and failure paralyzed him, until God sent people to help defeat those demons. The truth is, no one climbs out of valleys by themselves.

As a wife, I've always believed in his potential. I was tough on him at times, when I felt he was not living up to it. In his dark moments, I never let him wallow in depression.

If you ask him, I don't even let him lay down when he is sick. I would never lie to my husband, just to make him feel better. I give him the truth of the moment, which is hard for most men to deal with from a strong woman, but it's paid off. I've watched the valleys Cleon describes firsthand, and sometimes carried him through them. I guess you can call me his "passion protector."

What I love most is his compassion to help others. He draws energy from helping people change, by motivating them to wellness and good health.

Cleon reminds us we are all individually different and no two struggles are alike—but the formula of persistence and unwavering drive to increase and expand your influence is the same. The formula won't work when you quit. Tragedy, grief, guilt, setbacks and letdowns are the obstacles you either navigate through to make you stronger, or that cause you to fall to the wayside of mediocrity.

We want you to know you are not alone. Every mountaintop requires climbing from those valleys, up and down those hills. If you aren't making your way toward success, what is the point of living?

Read on and experience life through the eyes of a man who is in the thick of it. Laugh, shed some tears, and self-reflect (like I did with many others who read this work) as it relates to your journey. You'll find how much we all have in common in our desires to be successful. We hope you discover that your God-given purpose on earth is bigger than the want of material gain. Become lifted as you lift others.

We look forward to seeing you on your next climb out of the valley. We'll be waiting for you!

The Seed Was Planted at the Top

So here I am, a ten-year-old kid standing on second base at the start of the last inning of a championship baseball game. We were The Royals, and we were the defending champions. We were playing The Astros and had a substantial lead. The score was 17 to 10 and all we had to do was close out the game.

My father, also the head coach, called a timeout. Using father's privilege, he decided to have me close out the game as the pitcher. Simple enough, right? I convinced myself that the goal on the mound was to not mess up. Succeeding was the last thing on my mind.

He gave me a little shove toward the mound and yelled to me, "*Clee Clee, go close this game out champ!*"

Everything that could go wrong in that inning did. I was walking every batter, or they were scoring at will until the score ended up being 17 to 16. I found myself falling apart on the mound. That was my first nervous breakdown.

The baseball felt like a bowling ball in my hand. I could hear the crowd cursing and jeering me. These were not the just standard little league chants to disrupt my focus like,

"*We want a pitcher not a belly itcher!*"

"*Hubba, hubba, hubba, ring, ding, ding. Pitcher has an arm like a washing machine!*"

These jeers were comparable to bad performance at *The Apollo Theater*. The only thing missing was *The Sandman* coming out. I simply cannot repeat them.

The bases were loaded, and the home run king was at bat. This kid was six feet tall and everyone in the league called him *Frankenstein*. There was no way he could be ten years old. It was the longest inning ever.

I managed to get the call to three balls and two strikes, with both strikes being foul balls that measured the distance of a home run. With everything going on around me, I panicked and began crying profusely. My father saw my meltdown and called a timeout. I threw the ball down and ran toward the dugout.

While making my escape, my father who was standing at first base, intercepted and grabbed me. With his hand on my shoulder, he attempted to shake the panic out of me. When that didn't work, he used his backhand and lightly smacked me across the face. That reset me immediately, at least enough to hear his instruction.

I begged him to put another pitcher on the mound. I also told him I had a stomach ache. He shook me again and said, "Boy, you are going to march back out there and throw the damn ball!"

Having no choice in the matter, I walked back out to the mound. The laughter and jeers from the crowd were deafening. I could feel all of the frustration from my teammates. I could taste the victory I was about to hand my opponent, but I was more afraid of the punishment I would receive if I did not follow dad's orders.

I stood on the mound and gathered myself. I refused to open my eyes as I began to wind up for the pitch. At the crossroad of losing all hope, and having nothing to lose, I snapped the ball as hard as I could from my arm. I swear time stood still and I could no longer hear anything but the ball coursing in the wind.

The next thing I heard was the sound of the ball smacking into the catcher's glove. I then heard the sound of the umpire yell, "Strike three, you're out!"

All of my senses opened to pandemonium. The boo birds were falling all over themselves in anguish. The fans were going berserk in celebration. I looked to first base and saw my dad beckoning me with pure joy.

I ran as fast as I could to him. He embraced me, lifted me from the ground, and said the most profound thing anyone had ever said to me. He said, "Son, I don't care if you win or lose in life, I just want you to throw the damn ball!" His words reverberated in my mind with a heavenly ring.

At that moment, a life-long seed was planted. My father showed me that I have to take chances in life to succeed. Unfortunately, his mantra not only became a mission but became a life struggle for years. When I assumed the path to success in entrepreneurship, it was apparent, I had more to learn.

I am the son of an entrepreneur. Milton Joseph, who started as a factory worker, a janitor, and a postal worker, but grew tired of the "9-to-5" and decided to run his own ship. He, with the support of my mother Margie, became a successful "jack of all trades." He ran a grocery store, laundromat, construction business, real estate investing firm, and even a restaurant. I watched him make millions and eventually lose everything in the economic downturn of the '90s. My problems began there.

I was sixteen years old when my father decided to show me the finances of his small empire. He bragged about staying up on the times, and wanted to show off the best computer that the '80s could offer: *The Commodore 64*. That is where he showed me his accounting software. I wondered why he closed the door, as if he was trying to hide something. When I looked at the program, his books showed numbers I had never seen in a black man's portfolio, let alone on his computer.

That was the first time I realized we were well-off. He knew I would be shocked, because my parents always kept a humble appearance. They were influencers, but in my young mind I thought it was because they were just good-natured, respectable people. Although that was true, they had financial influence too. I knew we weren't poor, but I had no idea we were financially secure because of my dad's business ventures.

Now I understood why bankers and CEOs came to our home for advice. When he took me to banks or City Hall for loans or construction projects, everyone referred to Dad as Mr. Joseph. People of all colors and creeds sought him out, and with what I had just discovered, the puzzle pieces came together.

My father immediately explained to me that he was entrusting me to help him with the accounting because he felt I was responsible enough. I had an older brother who should have been in my position, but at the time, he was finding his own way. I think my dad was so frustrated with him that he was preparing me to be next in line. In my mind, all that was nice, but all I could think to myself was, *we are rich!*

In the early '90s, America was experiencing an economic recession. If you were smart, it was not the time to invest in anything. What made sense to me, with what little I knew about business at age twenty, was to hold onto your assets and wait it out. Not my dad.

In the midst of tenants not paying rent on the properties he owned due to their job losses, and already having to sell off a few properties to keep from going under, Dad had the idea to buy a shopping center with most of his liquid cash. His new vision was to have his family run it. We would operate a restaurant, a tool shop, and a loan company all by ourselves. We renovated a standing building and did just that. The problem was, we had no experience running a restaurant, nor a tool store, but my dad could do loans.

Before the tool shop, we had a potential grocery mart that wanted to lease the space where the tool shop was to be. My dad eventually turned down the deal, believing we would be better off if our family ran the center. I questioned why, because that would have paid the bulk of the shopping center mortgage, but he was adamant in his family vision and there was no turning back.

I helped run the restaurant. My brother, Deon, ran the tool shop (and flirted with the female employees of the restaurant or the other way around). My brother Troy was there occasionally (when he and dad were on good terms). My nephews and niece helped wait tables, and my mother took ownership of the restaurant. After all, it was in her name: Margie's Kitchen. My dad was the overseer of everything.

Despite our inexperience running a shopping center, the restaurant brand took off. We were in newspapers and magazines, meeting celebrities, and we won awards for our food. The problem was, we all struggled with the business side: inventory, thefts from employees, poor bookkeeping, and some not-so-reliable friends and family. On top of that, the economy hit so hard that patrons dwindled, while both of my parents were becoming ill.

My dad went from walking with the swagger that comes with being the "big cheese" to having debt collectors and investors show up demanding money. I tried to ignore that part. I figured my dad would fix it and we would be back on top. It even came to a point where my dad suggested I quit college and commit to the business. My grades weren't that great anyway, so I did.

I watched my dad spin into a state of depression. The last straw came the day he was climbing a scaffold on a job site (he was still active in construction) and fell and injured his back. I was concerned as a son, but I had never experienced watching a strong man break down. All I knew to do was work on the business until he got healthy.

My mother took over the best she could. She got no rest, working to exhaustion nightly. Things were really bad. As the business continued to fail, my mother became increasingly ill from overworking herself. Our restaurant business was a skeleton of what it once was due to the economy. I knew things were rock bottom when I saw her sitting in front of an empty restaurant selling children's school clothing that she hand made herself. She fell back to what she knew to do before the wealth. We call this in the black community, *getting our hustle on*. She was a supportive housewife thrown into business, doing what she knew best, on auto pilot, to survive. I stared in disbelief and shame. This type of grind was foreign to me.

She caught me staring and said, "Son we are not poor, we are broke. There is a difference and we have to keep moving."

I knew we were failing, but I was too afraid to investigate why—or did not want to know. My brother and I shared a house next to my parents, which they owned, but it got foreclosed on. When I received my notice about the house I ran to my dad's. He was broken, on the floor watching TV in his favorite spot, rarely moving because he was still healing from his injury.

I asked him what was going on.

He looked up at me and said, "Son, would you go to the store and grab some Jack Daniels?"

I was dumbfounded. I never saw my dad drink. He had stopped smoking when the doctor told him my brother and I had asthma in our toddler years, so this shook me. I refused to get him the alcohol, taking a moral stand. He told me he was in pain, but I still refused.

He sunk his head back on the floor and said, "I'm dead in the water and I don't know what else to do." For the first time, I saw him cry, and I did not know how to respond.

I went numb and became cold-hearted. I had saved enough money to get my own apartment, and so had my twin brother. It is fair to say I was insensitive due to fear. Somewhere in my soul, I believed my dad *(Superman)*, would bounce back. I left him there physically, and I left him there alone emotionally.

I don't know how they did it, but Mom and Dad recovered enough to revive the business. There was just one problem—the help had to go, and the help was my brother and me.

My parents decided to run a small mom-and-pop diner in a different part of the city. I remember closing out the restaurant with my mother when she said it was time for my brother and I to look for a job. Man, it could not get any worse than that. That would mean I'd have to move back home, an offer she left on the table for us.

We had no choice but to accept. Our family was falling apart, and everyone was in survival mode.

I thought back to a time when I had asked my dad if I could take a part-time job while in college, but he said, "I would never work for anyone but the family. Working for someone else is for the birds."

He always wanted his children to have a "boss" mentality, not a subservient one. Now my mother was telling me I had to find work. I was mad that Dad was not man enough to tell me himself.

When it came to employment, no one was hiring. My twin brother accepted a job delivering flowers, but he felt uncomfortable doing it. My older brother was making his own way; he and dad had fallen out once again. I even worked at a mortgage company, and when that did not work, I interviewed to become a tractor driver. I had zero experience.

Eventually, I took the walk of shame to the unemployment office. I remember pretending that I was looking for a friend, but there was no hiding my real reason for being there, at the front of the line.

All this time I was furious with my father, but he provided a roof over my head, so I kept my feelings bottled up. I thought, *If he would have let me be mediocre and find a halfway decent job when I had the chance, I would have been just fine.* Now we were all at the bottom.

To keep from falling into my own state of depression, I worked out constantly, training in martial arts. Then I went to my fiancé Eva's house (who would eventually become my wife), to feel a sense of independence from the shame of being an adult and living at my parents' home. Being the strong woman that she was, Eva grew tired of me lounging around and nagged me about getting a job. She even got applications for me, but I was too depressed to fill them out. I was *chillin'*.

No strong woman wants to see that in her man. So, she did the only thing she knew to drive me nuts . . . she nagged the hell out of me. If I slept on her couch, I woke up with a job application on my chest.

Everything was okay as long as the unemployment checks were coming in. But one day, as I was pumping gas into my car, the gas pump stopped at $7.42. I went to the attendant and argued with him, feeling something had to be wrong with the pumps. He was Asian. And since our community had just gotten over the L.A. riots, there was still tension between the Asian and African-American communities.

> *During the riots, many black people were upset about the Rodney King beating. The anger did not stay in the Los Angeles city limits. Tensions flared up across many cities in L.A. County, including Long Beach (where we lived). It was also a time where angry citizens expressed violence on other social issues in the black community. One issue in particular was the fact that Asians owned the majority of liquor stores and food marts in a mostly black populated community. It was the perfect storm for opportunistic rioters to act out all of their hang-ups.*
>
> *Neglect of resources and maintenance in the community by county officials led to slums. People were tired of being ignored. Stores were burned down, looted, and vandalized. People were being shot and killed. Asians were defending their property with shotguns (and rightfully so).*

While the arguing over my gas purchase continued, the Asian attendant pushed back just as hard as I did. The argument was over when he yelled, "You got no money! Now go!" He gave me a look as if he was bracing for a fight. He was not afraid of *the brotha*.

Assuming he would call the police, I chose to leave, but not without casually dropping the gas nozzle on the ground. I showed him.

I drove to my bank to have them verify my balance. These were the same bank tellers I used to flirt with, now giving me the look of shame. I knew

I had a few more unemployment checks coming, but I couldn't spend anymore until they came in.

I drove to Eva's house in the most gas-efficient way possible. She opened the door, and I fell into her arms crying like a baby. She gave me a shoulder to cry on momentarily, but that shoulder got real cold when she reminded me to get a job.

I said to myself, "Where is the love?"

I was at such a low point that I even drove to my place of worship, Antioch Missionary Baptist Church, and barged into Pastor Joe Chaney's office. I loved him to death and I needed to hear from a man of God. Plus, Pastor Chaney and my father had become good friends over the years.

> *My family left a church in my pre-teens somewhere in the mid '80s. Actually, my family was kicked out. My dad was a deacon there and apparently uncovered some mischief within the pastoral staff, and he publicly called them out. That caused a major blow up in the middle of a church service. Somehow the pastor convinced the congregation that my dad was in the wrong. The church believed the pastor, after all, he had the microphone.*
>
> *I remember everyone speaking in tongues, attempting to exorcise demons out of our family. That was an emotional blow to Dad, because he had completely remodeled the church, mostly out of his own pocket.*
>
> *Due to the pain of that experience, we stopped going to church for a year, until my mother decided enough was enough, and found Antioch. Dad became a deacon once again. Pastor Chaney and Dad grew a liking to each other, fast. Like everyone my dad met, I believe the pastor liked his boisterous*

swagger, yet kind heart. Like me, Dad can tell in a short time if he likes you or not.

It took me a minute to settle in at our new church. I had a hard time fitting in with the youth. I was already a nerd in school, so to keep from being a nerd in church, I stayed to myself. But Pastor Chaney was so welcoming and sweet, it didn't take long for me to feel at home.

When I entered his office after the incident at the gas station, I poured my heart out to him about everything.

Pastor Chaney took off his glasses, looked dead at me and said, "Now young Brother Joseph, your father and mother are fighters and so are you. I'm not worried about the Josephs. Y'all will be fine. There is something on y'all." He then read a scripture about the Bible character Job and how God allowed Satan to strip him of everything to test his loyalty. Due to his faith, Job was eventually restored. Pastor Chaney gave me a fatherly hug and walked me out of the office.

I was still angry, but I got my feelings out in the open and off my chest.

My dad eventually called my Uncle Roosevelt, who was a detective on the police department in Los Angeles. He was one of my favorite uncles, but I had not seen him in a while. My dad was trying to sell him one of his properties before it went under, but he also wanted him to talk to my brother and me about becoming law enforcement officers. I was a *wanna be* militant in my early college years. It was the early '90s and post OJ-Simpson-trial/Rodney-King-beating, and I hated police officers.

There was real tension between the blacks and law enforcement. The police took an extremely tough stance against drugs and drug offenders (dealers and addicts alike). The damage done to the black community in the '80s from the influx of crack cocaine changed the dynamic of community/police relations. Communities were destroyed, and it was left to police to fix the problem. Racial profiling was tangible (nothing like today's narratives—not even close).

I was stopped and humiliated a few times by cops. My Black Student Union at California State University of Long Beach did not help calm my anger. The Hispanic and Asian Student Unions were focusing on studying and exploring the world. We were mad. Don't get me wrong, there were some good things happening there also, but depending on the leadership, I was being indoctrinated to counter-hate. Aside from the release of courting my soon-to-be-wife, I'd wake up mad and go to bed mad at the police, and eventually, white people.

My parents never taught us hate. In fact, they kept the harsh stories of their experiences with racism to themselves, to keep us from being bitter. My parents raised forty-one foster children of all nationalities. We had one white foster child named Montoya, that Deon and I looked up to like he was our own. Mom trusted white neighbors to check in on us while they ran errands.

Having my uncle take us to the police station was all that was left for employment ideas at the time. My uncle, Roosevelt Joseph, urged us to go to the police station and talk to some of his friends. I believe he sensed the urgency of my dad to save my brother and me from taking the wrong path.

The ride was very awkward. All kinds of negative thoughts ran through my head. Were they going to search me first? Did I have to get beaten with a baton? Would I see those racist cops who beat Rodney King? But all of my stereotypes about police officers were shattered when I was introduced to his workmates.

First, I realized that there were a lot of them; and second, they were human, too, but had an ugly job to do. They were excited to see two black kids inquire about law enforcement. It was enough to convince my brother and me to take the test, pass it, and eventually get hired.

That was my saving grace. I was so desperate, I would have willingly signed up for the military, but the police department saved me. Hoping I'd learned from Dad's mistakes, I said to myself, "I have a job. I have security. Screw business."

Although I was at home helping my parents with the mortgage, we rarely talked. I loved them but resented them. In my mind, my life was held back by supporting the household while they revived their diner. Mom was killing me with her rules, and dad was always prodding to help him salvage his properties and take over.

Like a fool, I helped with my name but not my presence. Dad was not the strong man I once knew. It solidified my thought that a steady job was good enough for me. No more flying by the seat of my pants like I perceived my father doing at the time. I figured he was a grown man and would figure it out.

I eventually got married. My mother and father scaled down as much as they could and recovered enough to make ends meet. They gave up the diner and my dad slowly got back on his feet. He returned to construction and property investment. I don't know how he did it and I was too ashamed to watch and learn. I came close to losing everything while helping to save one of his properties. I had just gotten married, and my life and secure career had just begun.

Dad bounced back humbly, but that time was tough for us. I knew entrepreneurship was in my blood and I knew he wanted that for me, too. I was afraid of failure from watching what happened to him, so I suppressed it. I ignored how my dad came back from his valley. There was too much risk involved in taking chances in life. My new mantra was, "Job security is king."

I caused the ultimate self-inflicted valley by embracing mediocrity. My rise to my purpose was smothered by comfort, but not for long.

Your Seed Will Be Forced Out of the Valley, Like It or Not

I was relieved, working as a police officer, though never comfortable with the job. But it offered a guaranteed paycheck, benefits, and initially, a set schedule. There was always one thing that bothered me about the job though—you always did what you were told. It was acceptable when the orders came from someone you respected or who appeared kind, but when you had a jerk for a supervisor, it was agonizing. Most orders were not of bad intentions, they were purely day-to-day demands and missions of the day. You did what you were told, or you could be suspended or fired for insubordination. You could be nearly done with your shift and be held over, or you get that call of a serious nature at the end of watch and you were stuck for hours at the whim of your boss. It bothered me how much control a job had over your life, but because the pay was steady you went with the program.

When I worked the gang unit it was even worse; we had no control of our schedule. We worked at the whim of our captain and adjusted to each gang problem. I was proud of my work and proud of the people I worked with, but something was eating at me. Not having a say about my mission drove me nuts.

During my third year on the force, I was working on the west side of town and met this officer who was always reading MMA magazines. We began to converse regularly about cage fighting and it appeared this officer really knew his stuff. The friendship was sealed when I got sick while patrolling and had to go to the nearest hospital. I received a diagnosis of pancreatitis and had to be admitted. I remember being very disappointed while in the hospital because no one in my gang unit checked on me. I was hurt, until the officer I chatted with about fighting showed up and visited me. He told me he was going to Training Division to become a self-defense instructor for the department and promised if he could put a good word in, he would help me get over there.

Sure enough, a year later he called and told me there was a spot in the unit. I interviewed and got on the team. I thought to myself, *This is going to be great!*

I don't have to wear a uniform all day, I get to teach, and continue to stay fit and train hard on the department's dime. I can do this forever!

This job was right down my alley. I had been studying martial arts since I was fourteen, and at sixteen I began lifting weights. I competed in martial arts tournaments and discovered MMA during my first year as an officer. In the early '90s, I even competed in a natural bodybuilding show.

Outside of work, I was a fitness fanatic. I lived at the gym. Due to my physique and creative workouts, people began approaching me, wanting to train. It was an ego booster for me because there were other fit guys in the gym, but people were all coming to me. One of the head fitness managers, named Apollo, approached me regularly and asked if I wanted to learn to be a trainer. I gave the same answer every time.

"*Naw* man, it is too much studying and I don't have time. I already have a job." I was flattered, but my arrogance showed in my dismissive attitude. I knew I could outperform any trainer in that gym.

I spent so much time in the gym that it drove my wife crazy. Our marriage was still young, and looking back, I realize she just wanted my time. Whenever we went to the gym together, she would finish her workout in thirty minutes. As for me, I had an hour and thirty minutes left, and an audience who needed me. Eva would nag me afterwards, saying, "I would not be as upset if you were getting paid for all the advice you are giving."

I would be even longer in the weight pit at Venice Beach. I could be out there lifting, flexing and flirting for hours. For a while, my brother and I were treated like kings of the beach. When the beach staff saw us coming, we rarely had to pay to work out in the pit. We were an attraction. If it was not weight training, I was sharpening my skills in the early stages of Mixed Martial Arts. I was studying judo and jiu-jitsu. As good as it all was, the heaven I was experiencing at my new assignment at work would soon be short-lived.

It was the year 2000. It was fun teaching in my new job, but it was also competitive. All of the instructors seemed to want to be hailed as the most decorated instructor in the unit. When the rubber hit the road, it was clear the alpha teacher was the officer who got me the job. I'll refer to him as "Showtime."

He was in incredible shape, even better than when he was in patrol, extremely articulate, and had us all believing he was the master. He once said to another instructor that he had 400 fights and tapped out Brazilian jiu-jitsu black belts. He said he had high degrees in black belts I never heard of, but we believed him. His ability to verbally sell fire in Hades (about himself) magnified his prowess. I celebrated that at first, and I fell for the hype. He had the last word in everything self-defense, even over higher-ranking officers, and the supervisor took his word as golden.

In the beginning it was great, but I began to notice if you had the slightest difference of opinion he would verbally pounce on you, and sometimes physically shame you if he knew he could get away with it. Those antics got old really fast. As much time as I was putting in outside of the job, staying on top of the latest MMA and fitness trends, I started to feel that I had a voice too. Eventually, the verbal debates led to physical altercations.

To watch him intimidate others was becoming tiresome. The environment was no longer pleasant. I could always leave, but I didn't want to, the job still gave me joy.

There was one day in particular that piqued the decline of our friendship and the rise of our heightened rivalry. Whenever Showtime was having a bad day, he would take it out on everyone. Our supervisor did not correct him. In fact, he appeared to be entertained and encouraged it.

It was Friday, our open mat day, when officers who wanted to work out with instructors could do so. On that day officers could spar with instructors or work on learning how to better themselves in case they are in an altercation with a violent suspect. What was supposed to be light sparring with boxing turned into a punishment session for all instructors at the hands of Showtime. After our morning brief, Showtime accused everyone of slacking. He began ranting to a point of no return. Finally, one of the female instructors interjected. That did not go well. It was as if he was looking for someone to set him off. He demanded that everyone go to the mat room, with the supervisor's non-verbal approval, for some "training."

I'd had enough! I was training really hard outside of the job and my skill set was at a point where I could end the madness. I just needed a trigger. I first asked the supervisor if this could stop because it was no longer a professional environment. It looked like a gladiator session was about to take place. The supervisor would not engage me. After Showtime was warmed up from humiliating the other instructors, he called me into the sparring area.

I was already wrestling with other students, but I guess it was my turn. The spark for me was watching people get bullied. I looked to my supervisor, hoping he would step in and stop the escalation, but he looked like he wanted to see a fight. I accepted Showtime's challenge, because I felt there was no way out and I would have to end this today. I knew I could. I was getting my butt kicked daily by MMA champions and sometimes held my own with them.

I bested Showtime to a point where he did not look so indestructible. I brought his stature down, he was a great athlete with decent knowledge of martial arts, but he was also human, just like everyone else. I was athletic too, but it was clear who was staying on the pulse of combative sports and conditioning.

I did not take joy in exposing him. I just wanted the pressure to stop, and for a moment it did. Everyone in the room appeared relieved. It really hurt, because in friendlier times we were planning on starting a fitness business together, but at that moment, with his ego crushed, I knew there was no chance of that happening.

This incident was not pay-per-view worthy. We were both green, but I was becoming more experienced, and it showed that day. I had taken the metaphoric title, and the supervisor now sought me out for advice. Life was temporarily good again. Our boss even promised me a promotion if it were to come up. My wife, who was pregnant at the time, visited me at work and he told her the same.

I felt like "the alpha" (but a kinder version), no more bullies, and I was now the go-to guy. People listened to me for fitness and martial arts advice. I appreciated it, but I had no real credibility. I had never really tested my skills in a ring in a mainstream combative arena (with the exception of a karate tournament in my teens). I was embarrassed when people asked if I had a fight record. I was talented but had nothing to show for it. To solidify my credibility in my unit, I sought to resolve that question for myself.

There was a senior officer we called the "Blue Dragon" who competed in the '70s. Outside of him, no other instructor had any newsworthy accomplishment in competition—not even the bully. I threw myself into an amateur boxing tournament with the help of the Blue Dragon. He taught me the meaning of being functionally fit. I competed in grappling matches and I earned medals in each.

I learned so much that even my teaching changed. It went from a need to show how impressive I was, to an active teacher and coach who loved seeing people learn. I matured as an instructor. I was the go-to guy, and I thought nothing could take that away.

There is something about competing in a public place, where you are metaphorically naked for the world's judgment. I felt what it was like to win, and I tasted once what it was like to lose.

> In 2002, I signed up for a week-long amateur boxing tournament. I had a hard time making weight for heavyweight (one pound over), so they bumped me to super-heavyweight. I was

197 pounds and my first opponent weighed in at 270. He was so slow he could barely touch me. I even knocked him down. I won the match and my ego was through the roof. The crowd was going nuts. The second fight was with a 6' 8", 240-pound man (who was projected to win the whole thing). His prior match ended with his opponent severely injured from head trauma and taken away in an ambulance. At 5' 10" and all heart, I beat him also, knocking him down twice.

It was the last day of the tournament and I was excited to see that I had an opponent my height. I knew this was going to be a fun fight, but there was one problem: I was so excited about fighting that I forgot to eat at all that day. I was sluggish and tired going to the ring. To make matters worse, he was 240 pounds, with a stronger boxing pedigree than me. He looked chubby, but his punches were sharp. It was an ugly fight. This guy fought dirty. He knew how to hold and put his weight on me. I was winning the fight on points, but I had no energy in the last round. I could not even lift my arms. All I could think about was food. In the last thirty seconds of the fight he pulled off two major combos that gave him the points needed to seal the victory. That loss was frustrating. I was cocky and thought I could wing my way through, because I had already beaten the top fighter a day prior. I had visions of standing on the top rope receiving my gold medal. Losing, when you know you should have won, sucks.

It appeared that behind the scenes, Showtime and the supervisor maintained their personal relationship, as he stayed in the supervisor's ear. They were cronies. He even reminded everyone that I was a failure for losing the fight during the tournament. I did briefly ponder how a guy with no fights can tell another with fights that he is a failure. I had a job promotion interview scheduled, and I thought I did more than enough to earn the position. I was sadly mistaken.

Showtime also interviewed for the same position. I thought he was no threat because of his past antics. No one wants a temperamental hothead leading a professional unit, or so I thought. I gave the best interviews I could. I was told I was in the outstanding pool. Now I just waited for the official word. Everyone was on edge because most people did not want a bully on top, with the rank behind it. The next day, I got called into a room and was told by our supervisor and a lieutenant that it was close, but Showtime got the job.

I was completely devastated. I wanted this position so bad I began tearing up as I asked why I had been denied. They said though I was outstanding, the decision was made due to the "leadership matrix." Showtime had beaten me by a decimal point. The supervisor smirked as if he took joy in giving this bad news.

As I walked toward the door, I said, "If you guys don't want this, the world is going to get it." I left the room and said to myself, *Where did that verbal slip come from?*

As I look back, I realize I was never going to get that spot at that moment. In the eyes of key players, Showtime was a special individual.

In a corporate environment, many believe it is better to promote a problem than punish it. Maybe they think promotion will bring the individual to their full potential, that they will embrace leadership, or maybe they simply believe the person's talents are bigger than their faults.

Showtime sold himself, making leadership feel that our unit could not run smoothly without him. The outward appearance of our unit to our audience and students was more important than the turmoil inside of it. Showtime's game of "smoke and mirrors" worked well for him. My honesty and "grind" did not work for me. Sometimes, we have to accept that life works that way also.

I did my best to hold my head up. When I told my colleagues, the cloud of negativity came back. I went to congratulate Showtime. I was doing my best to be a good sport, so I extended my hand to shake his, but with a smug expression, he turned away. I had to absorb that, shamefully. Eventually we all watched the work environment change back to what it was before, a hostile state. And no one could say anything about it. This dream job was now a daily nightmare. I could not mask my disdain, which I acknowledged at that time.

What made it worse, was in secret, the supervisor continued to press me to help improve the unit or give advice. He prodded me for information as to what I was learning outside of the job and wanted me to continuously share my knowledge. Beyond that, I was alienated. Even worse, he sent his admin guy to become chummy with me, discussing techniques, so they could place my ideas in a new lesson plan, but purposefully left me out of the planning.

At one point, I was asked to help set up an off-duty self-defense curriculum, so our team could make money, taking the show on the road. I did the planning and established price points. Because I had once ran a business, the team looked to me for guidance. The problem was I had no idea they were going to leave me out of the action.

I discovered their plan from one of our civilian guest instructors named Mike, who eventually became my kick-boxing instructor. While having lunch with him, he told me how happy he was that we were going to travel on our own. I had no idea they had established a travel date. I never let on to him that I had been left out. I just took in all the information. The plan never worked, but I was later told that the team was concerned I would stand out because of my experience, so they decided to leave me out completely.

It was a baffling time for me. I was fed up with serving a boss at that moment. On workout Fridays, if I did not show any techniques, I was accused of being selfish. If I showed a technique, I was considered a show-off. But I found it really interesting that they would bring guest professional grapplers (some I'd wrestled against outside of the job), watching me spar with them. It was a win for them either way. If I was competitive, the unit looks credible. If I was dominated, it became their excuse to discredit me. (I rarely let that happen.)

Eventually, my unit was merged with our department's physical training unit to train recruits. I was shunned there too, because I was an idealistic. I was told I was too "out the box" in my fitness logic. I was now working in a unit of senior officers who had been teaching the traditional quasi-military way for years, and there was no need to rock the boat now. The standard push-ups, sit-ups, squats, running, and verbal thrashing recruits were the norm. Everyone was comfortable that way.

The supervisors of that unit barely wanted my input. I was working for another set of bosses with poor leadership ability, from my perspective. When they saw me coming, they knew I was going to present them with new ways to train recruits, using what I was learning on the outside, so they avoided me. But whenever they needed a presentation done, they ran to me. I had no control or creative freedom and realized that this was all what working for someone else would ever be. I knew I could not just quit, but there was something I *could* do.

The saving grace for me, was as long as my work record was clear of discipline issues, I could have an off-duty job or business. I became a certified personal trainer and it freed my spirit from dumping all of my passion into places that did not want my energy. My bare minimum was already excellent. My entrepreneurial spirit was pushing out from within. I began feeling like my father. Maybe he was going through a similar circumstance when he decided to start a business. Maybe it was worse for me because I knew, to a degree, my discontent was self-inflicted. Had I watched and listened to my father's lessons instead of running away while he pulled himself up, I could have avoided all of this. In the midst of this valley, I decided the world would get what I had to offer, on my own terms. It just wasn't totally clear how.

In hindsight, I realize the reason I was taken through this valley was not because people were bad or evil. (It is not that simple.) Sometimes, you will run into a group of people who are very comfortable with the status quo, and when you disrupt their comfort (even when needed) they will do all they can to ruin you. It is not personal—they just want things to stay the same. Other times, you'll have very talented individuals who made a name for themselves and who feel sharing the spotlight is a direct threat to their livelihood. They will magnify themselves even more, in order to dim your light. Sometimes, when the employees look to you for leadership more than to the leaders, that is a death sentence for your position. Then there are those who constantly pick your brain, only to steal your ideas for their glory.

Any of these scenarios present a problem when you have a greater purpose. You're not made to fit into anyone's group or mold. You decide whether to fall in with the crowd, get out before you are taken out, or find relief outside of employment to grow your purpose. It does not matter which field of employment you are in, if you are cut from the cloth of entrepreneurship, you will run into the same problem. There is even a story in the Bible about Christ having to "shake his feet" and flee the city because a crowd was hostile to his teachings (Luke 9:5). He was not loved everywhere he went. There were some places where people hated him and wanted to cause him harm.

My experience left me in a dark place, reeling emotionally, searching for answers. I prayed daily for some sign from the Lord to help me out of my misery. The God-inspired messages of inspiration were soon delivered in the form of human messengers and life lessons.

When you are going through valleys and you begin to find purpose, God will send messengers your way to push you in THE direction, but you may have to be at the bottom of the valley to hear the voices when they speak. We are most open to listen when we're down. We will never hear God's call when we are comfortable, because we are complacent and distracted by our present belief of what comfort is. I must have been in a real low place, because the messengers came loud and clear when I had nowhere to go but up.

I'll be honest, I was suffering a severe bout of depression with other issues in my life. On top of the drama at work between 2004 and 2007, my mother revealed that I had been molested by a family member. She told me she walked in on it, and the pain of her revelation angered me. I never found out what my parents did about it. I had to deal with that member as an adult, but I already knew that this person was molested at a young age, too.

Thank God I cannot remember what happened to me. I forgave—I had to. My twin brother's wife was dealing with the loss of her mother, whom I was fond of, so I could not vent to my brother about my problems. Her grief was so severe that he temporarily disappeared from my life in order to tend to her (and rightfully so).

I lost my mother on November 15, 2006, the day after my birthday, tragically, to a rapidly developing illness caused by a cleaning fluid she was using while doing house chores. She had lost her sense of smell years prior and used too much solution, which damaged her throat and lungs. For a while, she was functional though functioning from early stages of dementia. My father did his best to take care of her and he never let on to us how difficult it was.

I was training at the gym when my father called me from the hospital. He said, "She's cold." He could not bring himself to say my mother was dead. She had been in the hospital over a week and appeared to be recovering, but her heart could not take any more. When she first arrived at the hospital, she had me request that they not resuscitate her should she pass. Maybe because Dad was there, they made an attempt to save her anyway.

I was the first in my family to arrive. The hospital did not clean her body to make her presentable, so she was sprawled out on the bed half-naked, like a piece of meat. There was a police officer from Torrance standing in the room for the death investigation, and my dad was sitting in a chair holding her hand. I did not have time to cry; my brothers were coming, and I did not want them to see her body in that state.

Instead of my co-workers showing concern for my loss, one of the supervisors used my absence to show why I was not a leader. He wanted to make the point that I was scamming the city because I barely had any sick time left on the books. Maybe he forgot to factor in the time I used for bonding leave and taking care of my sick mother. Only a handful of the guys at work were allowed to show support at the funeral. This was not what police agencies were supposed to do to their people.

In our grief, we also had to keep Dad in good spirits. My mother and father were married forty-seven years, and his health faded so rapidly that my brother Deon eventually had to take him in. At this time, I was also involved as a witness in an internal hostile work environment investigation. I went from witness to main whistle-blower, and the blow-back was heavy. I was dealing with all that, and still nurturing the beginning stages of a fitness business.

That time frame was grueling. I learned when you cannot run to work to take your mind off your problems, you end up in a deep depression. You will question your existence when your whole world is collapsing. Thankfully, God sent human angels, and they were life-saving. While I struggled in the valley, God was orchestrating a sequence of events to literally keep me from disappearing.

During this period, I played hooky from church quite often. I was really angry with God. One particular Sunday, my wife suggested we go, though we were not really on good terms. My depression was a contributing factor to that. I was overworked, had young children, and honestly sucked as a husband. I had this young family and I wanted to pursue a fight career in my late twenties. There were times my wife really needed me, especially after two C-sections. I didn't understand fully what women go through emotionally after giving birth.

On top of that, our youngest daughter was sick, and we fought over how to care for her medically. She had asthma, eczema and severe allergies. I thought I was there, but looking back, I know I could have done better. I spent more time than I should have chasing my dream of being a fighter. I believe my wife developed a bitterness toward me and my ego. I found a way to blame her. We had so many disagreements that for weeks we'd go without talking to each other. I felt alone because I had no one to help lift me from despair, while everyone in my family was dealing with their own issues.

One Sunday, Eva woke me up and prodded me to go to church. I think she had had enough of us not communicating. I was so depressed I could not say much of anything. I just got dressed and dragged myself to go with her.

My first messenger was a man of God (how typical of God). Pastor Joe Chaney had passed away, and his grandson, Wayne Chaney Jr., had taken over as pastor of the church. When I did sneak into service, I loved the way he taught. He was an "out-of-the-box" minister, finding his own way in assuming pastoral leadership. He appeared to be fighting the same transitions I was fighting at work, except he was experiencing it as the leader. In his case, I believe it was the old-school leadership versus the new kid on the block.

There were no seats in the back of the church to hide in, so the usher sat us right in the front. The sermon he preached was not a message of hope and triumph. It was about the realities of the valleys in your life. I was taken aback by the sermon because it mirrored my current state. I was wide awake and lost my urge to nod off as I usually do (I forgot to wear my sunglasses that day). I waited desperately for the punch line. I was waiting for the answer. I did not get the answer I wanted. I got the answer I needed.

I still remember how he ended. He said, "For those of you who are struggling in the valley and all hope is gone, for those of you who have nowhere to go and you've done all you can, for those of you who are ready to give up and disappear from this world, my message from God to you is this . . . ."

We all were standing in the church. I believe he asked the congregation to do so. I felt my wife squeezing my hand. Although we were becoming more estranged at the time, her grip showed me that she was looking for the answer with me. Her hand felt like she was hanging on for dear life to our marriage. I felt myself squeezing back even harder in anticipation of the answer. For the first time in a while, our souls were locked in sync.

The Pastor continued, "My message to all of you is to wait." There was an immediate spiritual unravelling for both Eva and me.

My legs went weak, and for a moment I felt faint. Tears flowed down my eyes uncontrollably. If that was the Holy Spirit, I thank Him for leaving me dignified in my tears and on my feet. Nobody will catch me running down isles, rolling on the ground and screaming.

My wife wrapped her arms around me and began weeping with me. She is not much of a crier either, which made the moment even more intense. When the word *wait* came out of Pastor Chaney's mouth, it felt like someone slowly poured cold water on me in the middle of a desert. My mind raced back to the time I ran to Pastor Joe Chaney to discuss my father's valley. It felt like Pastor Joe's spirit passed on a redemptive reminder through his grandson.

Some of you reading this are probably in disbelief that the word *wait* was the spark to my entrepreneurial evolution. But I did not need motivational quotes. I did not need to hear that God was going to turn things around. I certainly did not need to hear that if I believed it, I could achieve it. I did not need to hear that everything was going to be perfect.

I was a week away from a complete meltdown, if things did not change in my life. I needed God's reality. Waiting was a clear instruction from God. It was the turning point for things to come. I trusted this message.

After my wife and I left the church, we took the family to the local buffet near our home. While eating, I heard someone yell my name. It was Apollo from the fitness center. A couple years prior, I turned down his offer to become a fitness trainer. I remembered how arrogant I was back then.

Apollo had a high-pitched voice, but it had a commanding tone, like my father's. "Hey Cleon," he said, "when are you going to stop playing around and get that certification?"

Thinking back to the sermon, I quickly asked what I needed to do.

Apollo said, "Man, I live nearby. Come by the house tomorrow and I'll tell you all you need to know."

It was uncanny, I was already scheduled off work the next day. The timing could not have been better. Without hesitation, I told him I would come by. I barely knew this man, but I had no reservations.

I stopped by his home and he led me to his backyard and showed me his home gym. He was on hiatus from the corporate gym, but he trained upscale clients out of his home. The set-up was amazing. It was a mini private studio.

Apollo wasted no time in getting me oriented to the role of a personal trainer. I remembered every lesson. He was high on himself, like my dad. He was small in stature but stocky and had swagger. He talked of himself in third person quite often. I looked on his wall at all the before-and-after photos of his clients. I was in the home of a fitness guru.

During my encounter with him, he never tried to offer me a job at the corporate gym where he worked. I couldn't anyway, with my full-time job. He offered to teach me how to be a trainer once a week, at no charge. That was strange to me. There had to be a catch, but I trusted the mission.

He taught me everything: body assessments, client behavior, motivational cues, and how to close a deal with a new client. He even walked me through the level of certifications I needed to add to my credentials. Doing the body fat assessment was a little uncomfortable, but Apollo was very authoritative. If you did not do something right, he would let you know in a very sharp tone. Like my father, he was former military, so I understood where he was coming from.

He became my mock client and I assessed his body fat as a man and as a woman. I used a skin caliper to pinch different parts of his body to calculate his total body fat percentage. I pinched his arms, chest and abdomen. When it came time to pinch his legs, it was difficult, because he was wearing sweats. He immediately dropped his sweats and was in his underwear. I was at a loss for a second. I thought, here we go . . . this ain't going down. I rapidly developed an exit plan. I was either going to run or prepare to fight.

He noticed my pause and immediately yelled, "Fool, calipers won't work on sweats! Now will you pinch my leg and get on with it, man." That chastisement made me feel relieved.

He also allowed me to assess his clients for practice until I got comfortable. After all the training was done, I asked him what I could do for him. He looked at me and simply said, "Be the best and pay it forward." I was dumbfounded.

I got my first certification and began training clients from work at different locations, freelancing. I was happy I had developed a new escape from the job, but it was tedious traveling for only a few clients. I needed a central place to train, but I refused to go the corporate route. I was always calling Apollo for advice and he was pleased that I called. To him, I had the fire, and he was very giving with advice.

I was still searching for a space to train when I received a phone call from Apollo a few months later. He said, "I need you to meet me at this gym in El Segundo. I want you to meet some friends."

Without hesitation I met him. He took me into a large warehouse that had been converted into an MMA facility. I met the owner and the fighter of the house.

Without me saying a word, Apollo told them, "I got this trainer, CJ, who needs a place to train. Are your rates still the same? Y'all know me. Apollo only brings the best. He trains jiu-jitsu also."

I was a little embarrassed by his compliments. I was a dojo rat at best; these guys were ultimate fighters. The gym was gritty, like a scene from a Rocky movie. It was perfect. Both men were pleasant, but naturally on guard.

It appeared they had trust in Apollo's credibility. They allowed me to rent space out of the gym, and I ended up training with some of the best fighters in the world. I had a place to grow my business and learn more about the human body through hands-on training. It was easier to take on more clients now that I was centralized. Word of mouth about me was spreading, and that was exactly what I needed. Apollo still had asked for nothing, and I was grateful. The gym was an escape and gave me something to look forward to after the mental frustration from work.

I ponder to this day how that connection happened—nothing but God working through people. My time in that gym exposed me to elite trainers and fighters. I learned by watching and asking questions. I also learned by jumping into the fire of MMA training. The growth was unbelievable, which led me to a higher fitness certification. It also led to the birth of my alter ego and business name: "CJ", CEO of CJ's Functional Fitness (www.cjffla.com).

And the messengers kept coming.

It was another hopeless day on the force. I was walking out to the training field with Showtime. We may not have liked each other much anymore, but we always had a mutual respect for each other's talents. There were moments where we were able to occasionally communicate in the same space, which I thought was strange. I guess we bettered ourselves as rivals more than we did as friends.

While we were walking, a really petite instructor from another unit ran up to me. I remembered her as a trainer from the academy when I was a cadet. Her name was CeCe. I never really knew her other than that.

She tugged at my arm and said, "Cleon, right? I had a vision about you!"

My vanity kicked in. I thought, *this is nothing new, I'm a good-looking guy.*

As if she heard my thoughts, she continued, "Oh no, nothing like that. It was a vision about you from the Lord. He has a message for you."

Not reading the passion in her voice, I simply said, "You're on the fourth floor, right? When we're done teaching, I'll come find you and we'll talk about it. Okay?"

She looked a little taken aback by my dismissive nature and told me she would be upstairs whenever I was available. I completely ignored the sense of urgency in her message.

As Showtime and I continued to walk out to the field, he turned to me and said, "You know Cle, I may not believe in a god, but if someone I barely knew had a vision from God about me, even *I'd* want to know."

I felt so stupid and stopped dead in my tracks. Then I turned and ran as fast as I could. I caught her before getting on the elevator. In the most apologetic way possible, I asked her to share her vision.

CeCe told me she was praying for healing for a nagging ailment when God gave her a vision of me kneeling at the foot of God, smiling, with my arms outstretched. It troubled her, because she did not know me very well. The vision was so vivid she felt she could touch it. She said I was glowing, in a peaceful state with God. God was giving her instructions to give to me.

I was blown away. I had been praying for God to send me a message that He was still with me.

She said, "God has given you the gift of fitness. If you follow his rules and don't fall prey to distraction, he will keep you and use you to help many."

I asked her what the rules were, and she replied, "I don't know. I asked God too, but he said you would know what those rules are."

When she said that, I thought of all the pitfalls of being a good-looking male trainer. I knew what the rules were.

Here was a woman I did not know personally, from another race, who worshiped differently than I did, giving me a message from God. On top of that, my rival was giving me common-sense advice. I thought, *What a God I serve.*

I felt reconnected to my God at that moment, and I caught the vision for how I would get out of the valley. I had my assignment, which helped me push through work, and I began teaching with more energy. But like most humans, I needed a little more confirmation. I needed a pillar of fire.

He Confirmed It In Spanish

Due to my law enforcement and martial arts background, I was able to find off-duty work as a bodyguard for music and movie award shows. It allowed me to save money to grow my business. I was sometimes on stage, sometimes escorting celebrities to their seats, or keeping a watchful eye at the after party.

I remember parking at USC and walking through the campus to get to the Shrine Auditorium for an event. I was looking very sharp, tuxedo and all. I saw two old Hispanic women conversing in Spanish. Both appeared to be in their 80's. One was clutching a Bible in her hand as if it were her most valuable possession. While I was walking in their direction, I began to ponder what CeCe had said to me. I began to blow it off as if she was crazy, and I fell into a mental rut while dwelling on the encounter.

As I passed the ladies, the woman holding her Bible grabbed me abruptly by the arm.

I was startled and looked her dead in the eyes, but her stare showed no concern for my alarm. She began speaking in perfect English, saying, "Young man, get out of your head and get out of the way of yourself. Let God lead you and trust him. You've been told." She held on to my arm and stared into my eyes a few moments longer.

I was stuck in a trance until she turned away from me, let go of my arm, re-clutched her Bible, and continued speaking Spanish to her friend.

I turned the corner to get to the auditorium, but I had to look back around and grab a second glance of the women. They were out of sight completely.

I knew the message was correct. I worked my shift with a new sense of energy. This was real, and I had to accept that my assignment had been given to me.

He Kick-Boxed a Message

During my time in my self-defense unit, I became addicted to every aspect of MMA. I wanted to learn everything. We had a department chaplain named Mike Wise, who also came occasionally to show us some kickboxing techniques. It was another discipline to take my mind off my problems. I was so impressed with him. He was very frail and unassuming but could pack a mean punch and kick with little effort.

I had to get to know him. He invited me out to the school where he taught, and the lessons began. He knew I was going through a lot. He could see it on my face and in my demeanor. Since he was a chaplain, I trusted him enough to share my life. Every kickboxing lesson turned into a counseling session. One day he laughed and said, "Haven't you had enough of being miserable? CJ, you are a killer during workouts, but you turn into an emotional wreck afterwards." That is when he disclosed his physical ailments.

He was suffering from a degenerative disease that caused extreme pain throughout his body. He believed his ministry kept the pain at bay enough to function daily.

After hearing his story, I immediately realized how small my problems were compared to his.

He told me that while we complain and whine like children, God still holds us to his chest as if we were babies, rocking us all until in time, we stop crying. The way he painted that picture of God sent a coolness across my neck and shoulders. The fight lessons eventually turned into spiritual conversations that slowly strengthened me.

A few years later Mike died due to his condition. I still don't have a name for what ailed him, but I was honored to be allowed in the hospital to say goodbye before they pulled the respirator from him. He looked so peaceful and was suffering no more. God took my friend in His arms and rocked him away from me, but the experience left me oddly encouraged.

While still dealing with the struggles of a negative season at my job, a new spirit was surging inside me. My passion for fitness grew more intense. I began to phase out the negatives around me and resumed my work ethic as best I could. I brought my passion from my assignment of fitness training to work with me. I was once again, excited about teaching in-service officers and police cadets, regardless of who and what was against me. There was nothing I could do to stop their animus (at least in my mind) so I took the title of "threat" from them by doing my best to water down my abilities, so I could be relatable to everyone. I soon learned I was excellent even when pretending to be mediocre.

One supervisor, a lieutenant named Mr. Charles Evans, took notice of my teaching ability. I recall walking in a hallway, and when he approached me, he said, "I heard a lot about you. I'd like you to come to my office to chat when you get a minute."

He had a good vibe about him, so on my first break I went to meet him. I had heard a lot about this man, and every time I saw him, someone was seeking his advice. Some called him a "think tank," and I found out why.

I walked into his office and he began to tell me how observant he was of my teaching. He was also aware of my troubles in my work environment. He was the immediate supervisor of the supervisors who were making life miserable for me. He said, "I heard a lot of good things and some crazy things that I had to check out for myself."

I did not know how to feel—had someone started another rumor about me? Was someone else upset at me for showing off or not showing enough?

He said that usually when that much attention is drawn to one person, where people admire him on one extreme and despise him on another, and there is no fault to find, that person must be "The One."

When he told me that, the weight on me momentarily fell off.

He said, "You are brilliant and there are some who don't know how to deal with it. You don't teach like anyone else in this academy. You inspire, and sometimes that can make enemies as well as admirers—particularly with superiors and senior officers who resist change. They are threatened by you, yet they don't know why."

I was taken aback by what he was telling me. Here was a superior on whom I could dump my problems, and he could save me from what was going on, but he had another concept in mind. One that would benefit me far more than the tangible problem in front of me. It reminded me of the Bible story about the woman at the well. While she discussed physical water with Christ, He was speaking of water in the form of spiritual enrichment.

Before I began to pour my heart out about my woes, Mr. Evans interjected and said, "Before we get into our discussion, I'd like to show you a few things that might be of value to you."

He had a way with words and a soothing tone to his approach that made you pay attention. It felt like he had been around the world a few times. There was an aura around him, I felt it when I walked in his office. One thing I noticed—all the books in his bookshelf were about leadership, self-reflection and inspiration.

He stood up from his desk and began drawing diagrams, formulas and quotes while lecturing me. There was a point where it appeared he was in two different spots in the room at the same time.

I had never met a human like this. He was on a different level of intelligence. My ears went deaf because my mind was racing to catch up to the brilliance in front of me. I was doing my best to look as smart as he sounded while talking. I sat up straight. I pretended to look like I understood what he was talking about. Truthfully, I could not grasp everything. There was too much radiance to take in. No human had left me as dumbfounded in a moment as this man had. It was as if I were standing before a prophet.

I snapped out of it the moment I heard something simple enough to connect to.

He said, "Cleon, do you read books? I have a book that I think you might like. It reminds me of you."

Without hesitation, I told him I wanted the book. When he handed it to me, I was expecting something on the same level as Einstein, but it was a small book titled *Jonathan Livingston Seagull,* by Richard Bach.

I was a little insulted, with all the talk of how brilliant I was, because the book looked like it was for children. I did not express my disappointment though, I just took the book and promised I'd read it.

I thanked him and stood up to walk out the door. He stopped me and said, "Cleon, as far as work, sometimes you can be the best and not be in your proper platform. Enjoy your book and be well. When you are done with that book I'll have another one waiting for you."

I left that office, ran to my car, drove home and began reading. I teared up profusely because he was right. The book was relatable to me. It took me a day and a half to finish it. I ran it back up to him in exchange for the next book.

Each book he gave me polished me for the next. I read books on critical thinking, leadership and psychology. I'd finish each book in days and run right back to his office for the next one.

The final book he allowed me to borrow was titled *Power vs. Force,* by David Hawkins. The first few chapters of the book were comparable to a quantum physics lecture. I had no idea how to process it at first. I almost stopped reading, until I had to take a long flight to Boston with the professional basketball team I was working for. I moonlighted as a bodyguard at the time for arguably one of the greatest basketball players of all time. Yes, another off-duty job to escape the problems in my life. This gig allowed me to travel across the country.

To kill time on the flight, I forced myself past the initial chapters and discovered the jewel of the book. It was about understanding what level of person you are. I discovered that I was on a high level of human development. It was the quantum version of Jonathan the Seagull. There appeared to be a code or riddle Mr. Evans was trying to unlock inside me with this book.

When I returned to work and ran the book back to him for discussion, I told him, "I feel like the book was a test, and the first chapters were gatekeepers to the meat of the book. Most people would stop at the first few chapters, and that would be the end of it. But those who push beyond the quantum lesson are granted access to a higher understanding of themselves."

It appeared he agreed with my analysis. My life was changed at that moment. I accepted that I was bigger than my current circumstances, and it was solidified that God had a platform for me to teach wellness.

When your guru comes, and he or she will, you will come to realize it often happens in the valley. You have to persevere. Mr. Evans was one of the most powerful messengers God sent to me. He clearly took a bite from the Tree of Knowledge and has not looked back.

In my worst moment in the valley—at the lowest point before going completely under—God sent messengers to sustain me. Because of their influence, I now knew my assignment and began climbing the path out of my circumstance to pursue the success God had planned for me. The seed my Father planted in me was blossoming. It was time to take some risks of faith and drive.

I've walked you through the spiritual beginning of my assignment, and now I ask you to allow me to share the tangible. I realize there are many who may read this work who do not believe in a God. If that's you, hang with me, I'm going to show you more of the practical. No matter your beliefs, I want to make sure you all get something from the flow of this work.

When in the Valley, Move or God Will Move You!

With the confirmation of God's assignment for me to become a fitness guru, I began teaching with more dedication than ever at work. Knowing I had a superior in support of my methods, I had the courage to push the boundaries of teaching without compromising lesson plans. When I taught recruits, I smiled, laughed, joked and encouraged, all without sacrificing my authority. Instead of the traditional "learn as you are told" method, I put the "why" behind the instruction. When it came to teaching fitness in the academy I educated recruits on what they were doing. I empowered them to ask questions. I used fun drills to get them to participate in the workouts, as opposed to making the training feel like punishment.

As a fitness trainer outside of my job, I realized that people sustain wellness when they are educated and entertained. Positive feedback is the key to lifelong fitness. The traditional method may get you in shape, but when you graduate (for many) the last thing you want to do is exercise after six-months of forced fitness curriculum.

I believed in infusing myself in the training, both with recruits and in-service, as opposed to barking orders and chastising from the mountaintop. Many senior instructors despised me for it. The test results were generally the same, but the absorption of learning was received in a more positive way. When it came to the self-defense portion, I had no failures as a lead instructor, which was rare. I taught my academy classes like I taught in the dojo or the gym. I wanted learning to happen in a free-flowing environment. My immediate supervisor, with a helpful earful from the more tenured instructors, treated me as if I was a trouble-maker. I did not do it their way, and almost everyone was uncomfortable, but as long as Mr. Evans approved, I kept pushing.

One day, I was called into a room with the captain of the academy and Mr. Evans. When I walked in, Mr. Evans was his usual calm self, but I knew something was not right. I knew exactly why I was there. I sat down and waited for the captain to speak.

Late Spring 2007

A few days prior to the sit-down with the captain, I was pulled into a mediation meeting with the two supervisors in my unit who were giving me problems. I was told that I was to attend a workplace mediation session. When the department identifies employees and supervisors who are not getting along, and a normal conversation will not fix it, the department calls in mediators to help re-establish a balanced work environment. During this session, all employees who have grievances can hash out their differences without fear of discipline. There is more freedom to speak freely, no matter the rank.

I was surprised by the mediation, because though I had been frustrated, I had used avoidance to cope with the problem. I was openly frustrated with the way things were taught, but I did not have any grievances to bear. Since I was in an environment where I was to express myself, I did just that. I received a one-day notice of the meeting, so I gathered all evidence needed to argue whatever came up in the meeting. I articulated my method of training, I physically demonstrated my methods, and I spoke my mind about the work environment to the mediators.

It was supposed to be a meeting between myself and the supervisors, but the supervisors brought in their "admin guy." I had no idea why he was in there. I was never asked if I could bring someone on my behalf. In fact, on that day, most of the employees had the day off. It felt like a setup was brewing.

I felt pretty good about the first half of the meeting. I addressed some of their accusations: me being late, my sick time, my teaching methods. I had documentation to dispute most of their arguments. Through the first half of the meeting the admin guy sat perfectly still.

> *The admin guy was a very interesting person. When he came to the self-defense unit he learned the curriculum like everyone*

else. Like Showtime, he bragged that he trained with these exotic martial art gurus you could never verify.

He was extremely articulate and had a lot of experience in his work. The supervisor at the time placed him in charge of keeping our lesson plan updated. He was very good at gaining your trust, but it was only to pick your brain to add ideas to the curriculum. Sometimes he would persuade others to confide personal issues to him, then he would use that to discredit individuals when he needed to stand out. Somehow, he even managed to receive a major martial arts award, although he was rarely seen practicing or teaching anything. To charm you, he would bring gifts and tech gadgets to seem impressive. Like Showtime, he had his way of getting by. He would gripe to you about a supervisor, and if you agreed he would tell the supervisor the gripe came from you. He was sneaky. Even Showtime referred to him as a snake.

When I recognized some of his antics I began to socialize with him less. I just could not trust him. For me, the friendship ended when he sold me a computer that was not working properly, and he refused to fix it. When I took it to the computer store to get it fixed, the technician wanted no part of it.

Things really went south when the supervisor asked me to demonstrate some new grappling holds so they could be filmed. We used my camera, but Admin Guy filmed and took the tapes. I asked where they were, but he never gave me an answer. This person could not be trusted. He was more sinister than Showtime. Showtime just wanted the limelight. Admin Guy wanted something more, and to this day I have no idea what it was. He was the supervisor's pet. He was with him all the time and got special perks. Those perks transferred over to the new *supervisors, along with the negative opinions of me. Under the radar he painted me as the bad apple to the new supervisors. I had no idea why he was threatened by me.*

As the meeting continued, I felt my arguments were getting through to the mediators, until the admin guy chimed in. The session became so heated it had to be stopped, with a promise of a second meeting. There were so many lies being told, with stories made up by him, there was nothing I could defend. I was angry and began to show my frustration. His accusations were so off-base, yet no one would say otherwise. It was a closed-door session, so anything could be casually thrown into the air of perception.

A third supervisor tried to keep things calm. My lieutenant also provided balance, but he could not take sides. The constant theme was that I was a troublemaker. Admin Guy made sure that seed was planted in the minds of the mediators. He took stories that were true, but the true culprit of those stories was not in the room. He casually affixed my name to those stories and it disrupted the tone of the meeting.

The mediators grew uncomfortable. Everything Admin Guy threw out there was effective in their minds. The meeting turned sour, so we were told another meeting would occur when cooler heads prevailed.

Now I was sitting in front of a captain being told I was being removed from the unit. There was no justification for it. I asked why, and he said the supervisors could not stand me. I was causing too many problems for the unit. I showed him my track record of no failures during the self-defense portion. I showed him that I had no disciplinary issues. I told him I did nothing wrong. He reminded me he was the captain, and his decision was based on keeping the peace. He reminded me that he had the authority to do so. He felt my problem was that I had a disdain for authority.

I felt like the meeting a few days prior was a set-up. I was told by a secretary that after that mediation, the supervisors ran to the captain's office and threatened to leave the unit if I was not removed. After the meeting including the captain, I was removed from the academy. There would be no further considerations.

That event sent me into an emotional tailspin. I was too tired to fight. I was too defeated to even seek legal counsel. I wracked my brain to find the message I was apparently missing. I did nothing wrong, yet I was punished. I had all the proof and documentation, yet it was not even considered. It appeared that when it came to internal disputes within the department, there was more freedom to move problem officers than when an everyday citizen complains about an officer.

I learned not to be so trusting with people. I also learned that if you do not document your accomplishments, someone else will take the credit. I learned not to show your cards until everything was in place. Later, those lessons helped me in my business. Ultimately, I learned it was time to get the heck out of there, like it or not.

I was told I might be reassigned to a patrol division, which meant I would be back in a squad car working twelve-hour shifts. I was told there was nowhere in the Training Division, where I had been working, to place me. I was considered too risky. They must have wanted me out bad, because that rarely happened, they typically moved an instructor to another teaching unit.

I was in a panic because I had no idea what my schedule would be under the thumb of a patrol beat. I thought of all the clients I would lose due to the dissolution of my cushy set schedule.

Out of nowhere, I received a phone call from a deputy chief inviting me to speak with him in person. It did not make sense, unless Mr. Evans had something to do with it.

When I sat in his office, the deputy chief told me he had heard about the work my twin brother and me had done for the department. He said, "I just left Personnel and Recruitment Section and heard what happened to you. Usually, in cases like this, the person is a little too talented for that spot. I think you could thrive as a senior lead officer in South Central L.A. or as a recruiter. Both roles could use a guy like you. Where would you like to go?"

I chose Recruitment Division. At that time, a recruiter could travel outside city limits, and I needed any chance to escape whenever I could.

I reflected on how humans could be so sinister. I believe now, sinister acts can help drive you to your purpose. They help create uncomfortable situations that push you away from what you think is comfortable.

I cleared my desk, gathered my things, and left for a completely different job within the department. I was told that one of the supervisors in the training unit was furious that I was not sent to patrol, but this was God's call.

When God wants to use you, He cannot have you in a comfortable state. He sends you signs, warnings, and sometimes trouble when it is time to leave. When you don't get the signs, He will move you—not the way man may want you to move, but toward His will. In my case, God had something better for me, and made it painfully clear it was time to go. I'm just glad I did not have to sit in the belly of a fish. You Bible readers know what I'm talking about. If you don't, read the book of Jonah.

It did not take long to get adjusted to my new job as a recruiter. The best part was that it did not interfere with my business. The schedule was even better than I had before. I made some great friends very fast, and my work ethic was appreciated. I also discovered that one of my bosses was also a fitness trainer and model: Cassandra Britt-Nickerson. I knew I was in a good place, with highly talented people.

The core of my job was to get as many people as possible to take the police officer exam. Creativity was the key to success in recruiting. I learned how to set up events and also learned how to better persuade segments of society to take action, regarding those who may be hostile to the profession. I learned how to be a good pitchman. I became a familiar and welcomed face in colleges, churches, and community centers where only a few other recruiters would feel comfortable doing their jobs. They even made a poster of me and placed it in malls, parks and other public spaces. I learned how to do radio interviews and public service announcements.

The African American market was an extremely tough demographic to recruit, back then. Historically, the black community had a legitimate mistrust of law enforcement. I did not let that discourage me.

As a recruiter, I worked twice as hard to ease the pain and embarrassment of my prior assignment. Plus, it allowed me to be actively involved with the public we served, in a more human and engaging fashion. I was very successful recruiting in a difficult market. I was getting so good at public speaking at major events that former gang members thought they had a chance at employment.

My lack of fear when developing new avenues of recruiting led me to a local Los Angeles Rhythm and Blues radio station called Radio Free 102.3 FM KJLH. They had not worked with our agency for a period of time due to budget cuts.

One of my partners double-dared me to go into the radio station and meet with the sales agents. I was up for the challenge. I walked into the station and marched right up to the reception desk and asked to speak with sales to discuss our recruitment efforts. I was in full uniform, and the receptionist was momentarily startled. A lady by the name of Rochelle Lucas came out and spoke with us. She was very welcoming and brought us into her office. I enjoyed talking to her as she showed me her current advertising prices.

Due to another economic recession, the station was offering unbelievable rates for advertisement spots. She gave me a packet to read and I thought to myself, *Even I can afford these rates.*

When I listened to the radio, they had commercials marketing their "economic special" for advertisers. The prices were unheard of. The recession was so bad that many businesses stopped advertising, so I guess they had to do something. I told her I had a fitness business of my own and asked if it were possible to meet with her to discuss my own efforts.

Weeks later, we met. Everyone won in this case: recruitment was able to fit radio advertising within their budget, and I was able to grow my fitness brand in an untapped platform. I was ready to invest money to get my brand on the map. It was a financial risk due to the economy, but I had to roll the dice. My only safety net was the fact I had a job which was not going anywhere. I needed my brand to get out, and word of mouth could only take me so far. (Sounds like something my father would say.)

I had saved for this moment, so when it was time to pay the radio station, I paid in full. Rochelle looked at me in shock, as if no one did that in the recession, but I had to. That was the only way to fully commit.

I sat at home and wrote my own commercials. I wanted them to be different from anything previously heard over the air. The commercials being played at the time were redundant, due to the lack of advertisers. The dead space was filled with public service announcements. It was the perfect storm for something new. The world was about to know CJ of CJ's Functional Fitness: "You don't have to be a fighter to feel like one. So, let's train!" (www.cjffla.com)

I met with Rochelle and the studio engineer to record the commercials. When I shared my draft with Rochelle she was impressed with my efforts but wanted to utilize a more standard format. I was adamant about not changing my concept, but I did allow her to help polish a few minor details. The three commercials we produced only took a few takes. The engineer was impressed, and even entertained, by the energy. I think even Rochelle began to understand what I was doing.

We set a date to launch the commercials around my upcoming vacation. Since I was still renting space at the gym in El Segundo, I simply offered private training sessions and a Boxing DVD that I had made with a few clients.

During that same period, I had more money to invest in myself. I had saved every penny I could during the hell I went through at the academy. My determination to honor my verbal promise to share with the public that which was unwanted at my job had consumed me. Now, I was making it happen. But like my father, I picked the strangest time to throw money into a business like personal training, considered by many potential clients as a "luxury item", something usually removed first from a consumer's budget. I pondered whether that was what made my father do the same for the restaurant business.

The economy was so bad, that while driving on the freeway I noticed dozens of billboards with no advertising on them. I drove to the academy and saw a clear billboard right over the entrance of the academy. It was within radius of the local radio station and the gym in El Segundo. I found the company responsible for the billboard.

When I called, the agent was shocked. She told me how slow things were. I asked her the price of the billboard and she, like Rochelle, gave me the economy special. The difference between the price that was paid for a standard billboard and the price I was quoted during this recession was mind-blowing. Not only was it more affordable than expected, but the agent offered an extra month at no charge. I sent her my graphics immediately and paid in full. I was now about to run a radio campaign and a billboard campaign at the same time. I may have taken a huge financial risk, but I felt alive. I even spent top dollar on a state-of-the-art website.

My job at recruitment also began making large banners to hang over the academy. There was a local indoor football team, the Avengers, that partnered with recruitment for advertising. They used me as one of the models in the recruitment banner. I found out that the banner was going to drape over the academy entrance, directly under the billboard I purchased. It was the perfect set up for my climb out of a very tough valley.

Kaboom!
We Have Arrived

During my vacation from work, there was no rest for this weary officer. I dove into my daily business, but at least there were no time constraints. I could do as I pleased during my vacation and working on my personal endeavors gave me satisfaction. For a down-turned economy, my fitness business was good. Word of mouth marketing was proving effective. Ironically, my clientele mostly consisted of workmates from the academy and their references. Some members of the self-defense unit sought me out on the weekends to train them. Some wanted fitness, and some wanted grappling lessons. The goal was simple: make enough money in one month to quit my day job. The audacity of me.

I called one young officer who trained in the El Segundo gym with me, "Hurt Locker". No matter how well I fared in sparring with him, I was in pain for days afterwards. A great wrestler in his own right, he absorbed everything I taught, and I learned from him also.

We were first introduced when he came to the unit. He'd stop in as a patrolman and wrestle with me on open-mat Fridays. He started out a scrappy 185 pounds, but once he joined the self-defense unit, he rapidly gained weight, though not in a good way. He was soon 230 pounds and obese. He hired me as his trainer to help get him in shape for a wrestling tournament. In a few months, we brought his weight down to nearly 200 pounds. While training, we discussed how to make the curriculum at work better. It seemed like the supervisors listened to him and were more comfortable accepting information from him than me. So, I shared ideas that he embraced and took back to the unit.

We became like brothers. Although he was white, being raised in a black neighborhood gave him an urban edge.

When I was removed from the unit, he became the go-to guy. Everyone respected his opinion and instruction. He helped sneak a lot of my concepts into the curriculum. I did not care who got the credit. I was just happy our law enforcement training officers were on the right track and were receiving more realistic and safer lessons. He was pivotal in keeping my fingerprint in the system during my absence. The integrity of officer training was still important to me.

One day, I left the gym in El Segundo exhausted. I was driving home and heard my commercial on the radio. The fatigue I felt immediately turned into indescribable joy when I heard myself on the airwaves. I had done interviews for recruitment at the radio station, but this was different—this was all me about my business. My wife heard it too and was ecstatic. My phone rang off the hook with well-wishers, particularly from people from the academy who knew what I had gone through.

I could not sleep that night and kept the radio on to hear the commercials. I drove my sleepy wife crazy (in more ways than one).

In the morning, I got up and headed for the academy bank to deposit some client payments. On the way, I received a phone call from my academy friend, CeCe. She said, "Cleon, there is a billboard with your shirt off over the academy. Everyone is going nuts!"

I began receiving more phone calls from other people who were in my corner. Another friend called and said, "Hey CJ, there is a police department banner with your face on it for 'The Avengers.' How ironic."

I was so anxious I probably drove over the speed limit to get to the academy. Hurt Locker also called me and confirmed the same.

I got off the freeway, made a quick left and took a straight shot to the academy. Everything moved in slow motion. I could see the billboard and the banner on the horizon. The view was majestic. As I was pulling up, I heard yet another radio commercial of mine. I was overcome with emotion.

When I went into the academy, I was greeted like a champion who just won a title fight. I did not realize how many people were so jubilant in this moment. They knew the story of how I was removed, and embraced the moment of vindication, as I did. The platform Mr. Evans spoke about was taking shape. I will be honest, I took momentary pleasure hearing about the anger of the supervisors and others who were not fond of me.

Some employees searched to see if I was out of compliance with department policy. I heard someone else even tried to claim I was naked on the billboard. But there was nothing they could do but take in all of that *nakedness*. I already did my research in anticipation of any negative actions toward me. That was enough for me to let go of the pain, forgive all, and move on. Well, after I purchased another billboard near the freeway on-ramp, so my haters could see me naked again on the way home from the academy—then I moved on.

Today, I am grateful for the people who helped push me toward the real me, the supporters and the naysayers or *haters*. These obstacles (in the form of humans) were not evil; they were simply comfortable where they were and they either had rank, status, or motive to keep a job that controlled their livelihood. The status quo was good enough for them. I get why they were upset with me.

Change is difficult, complex, and tedious when people selectively reach their limit of growth. They do not understand an entrepreneur's mind, but vision is difficult to contain. I eventually learned how to balance this issue, which I will share later in this book. Trust me—it will make your life easier.

After my first marketing campaigns, I began receiving emails and phone calls. It started with well-wishers, then people from the community, churches from around my neighborhood and places I recruited in. I loved it when people were able to figure out that the man they called CJ over the airwaves was the same recruitment officer they knew. I also used social media for marketing, but now that I was receiving so many friend requests, I had to start a page for my business.

Soon after, client inquiries rolled in. I received a phone call from Rochelle, telling me how popular my radio spots were. People were calling the station looking for this new fitness sensation named CJ. I loved being in the moment of what was happening, and I felt like an instant rock star. But the real work was about to begin, because I had to make back the money I had invested, and fast. Business picked up to a point where I needed a facility to call my own, but obtaining one would require walking through another valley.

The Valley of Implicitness: Good Credit Ain't Enough

I find it perplexing that I have to discuss implicit bias in 2007, let alone in 2017. In the heyday of my dad's success, he constantly reminded me that your credit will get you past your appearance.

In 2007, we were about to embark on electing the first black president in America. In my mind, to have that happen would be the final blow to the negative perceptions of people of color. I was hopeful because so many cultures got behind the bi-racial presidential candidate. I chose to be optimistic with blissful ignorance, but that notion was challenged when I wanted to lease my own studio. You still needed good credit, but as I discovered, in some small cases, people's stereotypes of you may be a deterrent. I wanted to be wrong about this, but the facts made it very difficult to suppress that reality.

My time at the MMA gym was slowly coming to an end. One of the trainers who had been there long before me, an Olympic lifting coach I'll refer to as Big Sean, had a falling out with the gym owner. The tension in the gym became thick as Southern humidity. Eventually, he left the facility and leased his own place inside of an industrial area near my home in Lawndale. He called me immediately and told me there were more spaces available. When he told me the monthly rent amount, I could not pass it up.

Where I was currently training at that time, there was no cap on rent. You had to pay a fee per session. I had so much business that when I did the math, I found the lease Big Sean was paying nearly matched what I was paying in the gym. I might as well have leased my own place.

I had watched and become acquainted with another trainer in the gym named Kelvan Gamble. Everyone called him K-Flash. He was a former track-star-turned-trainer. We were becoming good friends, more so because I loved his work ethic.

I was especially interested in his unusual success as a black trainer. I remember the first thing I said to him. "Hey Kel, how in the heck did you get all these white clients?" It was just the ice-breaker I needed to chat with him. My dad used the same type of humor to charm people.

> *My father was a very outspoken man even in humor. He used "zingers" to get in and he knew exactly who to "zing."*
>
> *I remember, in my childhood, Dad walking up to a fellow contractor while bidding for a construction deal. My dad stood at 5 feet 6 inches, with a stocky build. The competing contractor was 6 feet 2 inches and built like Hercules. In the middle of the bidding my dad walked right up to him and said, "You get this bid over me, I'm gonna whup you're a**!"*
>
> *I was ready to find a place to hide because I was sure Dad was about to get beat up. But the giant of a man paused, looked at my dad and gave the heartiest laugh. Before you knew it, the man was at our house playing dominoes.*
>
> *One time Dad took me to City Hall in Long Beach to drop off plans for approval. There was this one very overweight white man behind the desk. My dad gave him the plans and began to walk away. Out of nowhere he turned around and said to the man, "You are about the ugliest son of a gun I ever saw!"*
>
> *The planner laughed out loud and replied, "Mr. Joseph, we love you too!"*
>
> *There is no way I could get away with that.*
>
> *At best, I'm good at finding contrast in my humor to break the ice. The one I thought would get us both jailed was when Dad walked up to an overweight bank teller and said, "Woman! It would take four arms to give you a hug, but I'd have fun*

trying." The reason I was concerned was because she was white, and it was the '70s.

That woman blushed, chuckled and said, "Mr. Joseph, you are such a big flirt."

K-Flash fell out laughing with my introduction. My question about his clients was the perfect lead in, so I could get to know him. But I seriously wanted to know his secret. His clients were doctors, lawyers and real estate agents. During our conversations, he told me he even traveled with some of his affluent clients who happened to be white, to exotic vacation spots.

As for my clientele, they had similar professions, but were mostly African-American and Hispanic. My clients reminded me of my community growing up, and I had attained them from my advertising on the legendary Radio Free station, with a listener base that was mostly black and Hispanic. I was just happy to have great clients—it did not matter where they came from. I was proud of that, but I wondered if I was lacking diversity or if white people were scared of me.

One of K-Flash's clients told me I looked scary when I trained. She said I wore a very intense expression when working, and I absorbed that in a positive way. I appreciated her candor. As my business grew, so did the diversity.

K-Flash and I continued to watch each other work until we both got the nerve to discuss leasing a studio for ourselves. He had a heavy client load and lacked a rental cap like me, it was hurting him also. When I told K-Flash that Big Sean called and told me about a spot in Lawndale, we jumped on it. The three of us, along with another trainer, tried to get a warehouse in El Segundo earlier but were unsuccessful, so it was nice of Big Sean to think of us.

I called the leasing company and scheduled an appointment to see a unit. When I called, I disguised my voice, so I did not sound *so called* black. I learned that trick from watching my older brother, Troy, when bidding for construction projects for my dad and himself. I did not want to take any chances, so I used his gimmick. It got me the appointment. I told K-Flash the date and time of the meeting, and off we went.

I got to the location on time with my wife. I am obsessive when it comes to punctuality. I was dressed business-casual. My wife had just left from the school she was teaching, so she was already prepared. I stood in front of the studio, waiting for the leasing manager, when a motorcycle pulled up.

Once the helmet was removed, I recognized K-Flash. He had a do-rag on, white T-shirt, and sweats. I was fond of him, but not cozy enough yet to express my concern about his attire. We were all standing outside, wondering why the manager was late. At the same time, we kept seeing this luxury sedan circling the location. Each time the lady passed us, she would do a double-take. After the third pass, I realized it was her.

I guess she accepted the fact that we weren't disappearing anytime soon, so she parked her car in front of the unit, sunk in her seat, and took it all in. I already knew what the problem was. It was K-Flash, at least that was my first thought.

I could tell by the slump in her posture that we were not her typical potential tenants. The woman took a deep breath and exited the car. Her bad energy hit the three of us immediately. She looked like her time was being wasted as she opened the door of the unit and said, "Well, take a look."

We walked in and checked out the place. It was perfect. We noticed however, the manager never came in. I assumed we'd get a guided tour. *Maybe she had to take a phone call*, I thought.

I walked outside and saw her sitting in her car. I said, "We are interested in the spot. Were you going to give us some details? We have questions."

She got back out of her car and walked in to the unit. My wife is a very passive-aggressive person, but the scowl she gave the manager was priceless. K-Flash was cool as a cucumber, but he had a way of chewing his gum when he saw B.S. and it was all coming in loud and clear.

The manager quickly gave us the square footage, the security deposit information and monthly rent, plus common area maintenance costs. I told her we were interested. I did my best not to show my anger. I needed a space, and this was a test of patience in the face of being judged by appearance. I felt it was no different than when I bought my last two cars. I thought my high credit score would fix any apparent assumptions.

> *Early in my marriage, I went into a dealership to buy a new car. I wore casual clothes, and of course my wife was looking her usual dignified self. We waited in the showroom much longer than needed. We could see all the dealers hesitating to approach us. I had been through this once before with my very first car. I understood it then, because I was young, but did not understand it the second time around.*
>
> *Finally, when they realized we were not going anywhere, a saleswoman came out. She was not rude, but she wanted to make our visit quick, so she could find a more serious buyer. I asked her about the zero percent financing for the utility vehicle that I wanted.*
>
> *She chuckled and said, "That is for people with excellent credit."*
>
> *I said, "I don't think I would be asking you about the zero percent financing if I did not qualify."*
>
> *She hadn't even shown the car, but asked to run my credit. I obliged her.*

> *Within minutes, she and the manager came running out of the back office with smiles. The manager said, "Mr. Joseph, I just wanted to come out and meet you personally. My sales agent is going to give you the best offer possible."*
>
> *I went from having the plague to "Mr. Joseph," meeting the manager, all on a credit inquiry. My credit was my ace-in-the-hole when my pigment was failing me. Some of you reading are probably wondering why I did not go to another dealer. But out of the three dealerships I went to that day, they were the best of the worst when it came to customer service. The dealer before them was cool, but he kept pushing these pimped-out cars. I did not want furry seats and oversized rims. Once they saw my high credit score, the focus became more on my ability to pay, not my color.*

Later that evening, the leasing manager of the property emailed the rental application. I sent a copy to K-Flash.

Although we were two separate businesses, the objective was to split the rent. K-Flash was upset that she did not send him the email, feeling completely dismissed.

The document was at least four pages long. They were asking for five years of business tax returns, four corporate references and more verification documents than was reasonable.

First of all, K-Flash and I had none of that. Both of us were establishing a place to operate our businesses for the first time. I had already sent my credit verification form. I thought we would be fine after that, but I was wrong.

I was having trouble understanding parts of the rental application, so I called Big Sean, who would be my neighbor across the way if all went well.

Big Sean looked at the document and had a confused expression on his face while his cheeks flushed. He said, "I don't know what the heck this is." He immediately became upset with what was happening to us (one of his many noble qualities). Big Sean had moved into his unit a month prior to our walk-through.

I said, "Are you sure? Didn't you have to fill out the same document?"

He told me, "Come see my application for yourself."

I went to his studio and reviewed a copy of his rental application. I could not believe what I saw. It was two pages. There were no tax inquiries or requests for corporate references. For some reason, I was relieved, because I had a feeling I was going to get denied the unit. Big Sean's document gave me the ammo I needed to seal the deal.

I called my mentor, Mr. Evans, (I thought he knew everything), who advised me of the different discrimination laws I could cite in case I needed it. I also consulted my mother-in-law, who was in real estate. Behind the scenes, one of K-Flash's clients, who was also in commercial real estate, white, and now angry for us, drafted a letter filled with jargon that a fellow agent could understand to help curb the behavior that was being exercised on us.

I called the manager and playfully asked to go over every line of my rental application. She swore all of the tenants had to fill it out and it was standard. She even sounded hostile because I dared to question the details.

I let this go on for a few more minutes, then said, "You know, I saw the rental application of one of your newer tenants. Why is it so much easier to understand?" I fibbed a little and told her that I door-knocked other tenants and saw theirs. I took pure joy in hearing her walk back the lies.

She did her best to cover her tracks by saying that this was a new application, but I reminded her of what she told me about the standard. I stayed quiet on the phone and let her ramble until an apology was given, saying she made a document error. She pleaded with me to accept that she'd simply sent the wrong document. We got our unit—motorcycle and do-rag included.

Today, I'm not as quick to call a person a racist. I learned with my tenure in life, a new term just below it. It is called *implicit bias*. The concept implies that bias is a deep-seated, learned behavior. It is the type of behavior which leaves a door open for education. I would continue to educate this manager for years to come.

Months later, I asked K-Flash, as we got to know each other more, about the dress attire he wore that day. He told me that where he was from and the experiences he's had, the clothes don't make the deal. He jokingly reminded me that I once asked him how he is able to get white clients.

I had to absorb that and accept my perceived bias with K-Flash's dress attire. I immediately reviewed in my mind all the business deals my dad made in his racquetball shorts, with people who did not look like him. I also remembered the ex-cons, former homeless and recovered drug addicts my mother and father helped get on their feet, who are still successful to this day. One of the valleys I had to overcome was implicit bias. We all have it. But what happens when your valley comes from doing everything right and you still run into more valleys?

Just keep reading.

Leave No Stone Unturned in the Valley

There was only one problem: The City of Lawndale. With rental agreement in hand, I got the keys to the unit, paid the security deposit, and gave a copy of the key to K-Flash. I was never told I needed a special permit, until we were close to signing the agreement. Due to our minor issue earlier, we were given a little more time to obtain a permit before signing the lease. Later, I found out two other gym facilities in the same complex, one used as a strength and conditioning gym for volleyball, the other an abandoned space next to ours, had no special permits.

I could have conducted my business like everyone else around me, without getting the required permit, but after my experience just trying to obtain my unit, I did not want to take any chances. I went to City Hall and immediately met with the planning section.

I met a woman who advised me that for the zoning area I was in, I was not permitted to have a gym. I was frustrated and wanted to tell the woman there were two other gyms operating with no permits, but I felt that would be wrong. They were none of my business, so I kept their missing permits to myself. I simply asked if there was anything I needed to do to change my circumstance in getting the permit. The woman kindly advised that I needed to attend a hearing. She also told me I needed to get the land surveyed and draw a diagram of the location. The cost was a few thousand dollars—that presented a problem.

I had put most of my money into the security deposit and had just enough money to throw one more billboard up at a major intersection near the gym. The permit requirements wiped that plan out. I took my marketing money and paid for the survey and hearing. There would be no refund if we were denied, leaving us stuck with a gym we could not operate.

I felt I should not have even come to City Hall, they wouldn't have known what I was doing. We could have done this on the slide; other gyms were getting away with it. Deep down inside, I knew I would have gotten caught. I am one of those people where Murphy's Law always applies. Anything that can go wrong will go wrong if I don't follow protocol to perfection. So many people I know are good at sneaking through life and getting lucky, but not me. Things always come back to haunt me when I misstep or take the easy way out.

I felt a sense of comfort because the woman assured me that it was not a big deal and most people get approved. With the faith of a mustard seed, I continued to move equipment into the unit, while still training some clients and teaching the boxing class at El Segundo. K-Flash and I wanted to wait until we knew we had a space before we told the management there. I was on good terms and was still hopeful that we could keep a relationship with them.

A week went by and I heard nothing about a hearing date. I went back to City Hall and this time was met by a male. He advised me that the lady I was working with was on leave and he would be taking over my case. He gave me my date and I turned in all the information they needed. While waiting for my hearing, I made sure I paid for all of my insurance. I went to my tax person to make sure all ducks were in a row. This is how I kept myself occupied until the hearing. I was told that I could bring some clients to speak on our behalf that day.

The day arrived, and we were set to pitch our business to the city council. My case agent, the male, did one of the worst logistical presentations I'd seen. It was like he wanted it to fail. I had a copy of the presentation and caught him misspeaking on some crucial data. I could no longer let this continue.

With passion, I took the podium to clarify everything, showing where the case manager was in error. I only had one shot and I was not about to let some guy ruin my plans. He glared at me to let me know he was upset with what I was doing, and I glared right back. After the brief stare-down, I looked to the council members. They were very engaged, yet I could not tell if they were upset that I interjected or appreciated my passion.

The elder councilman asked if I brought references, and if so, said I could bring them to the podium. A client named Dawn shared her weight loss journey. She had lost 80 pounds over time with me, but also disclosed how her life had changed since losing the weight. Her story brought one council member to tears. Others were smiling with approval. More people were lining up to speak, and I was welling with pride. To hear my brand being described with words like professionalism, excellence, and strong work ethic meant the world to me. K-Flash brought some of his people, too.

The council had heard enough, and it was time for a decision. We needed at least four of the five members to show their green light of approval. That part took forever, and each second was agonizing to sit through. The lady who was brought to tears gave a no vote. I was perplexed; I knew I had her vote in the bag. I was upset and defeated because I had done the right thing. Those other gyms did not, but I had. The next three turned green in my favor and then there was one more vote.

> *At the El Segundo gym, I was training a best friend's girlfriend, who was an up-and-coming trainer. Her name was Chai. What she appreciated about me was my professionalism and my impartiality during a rough patch in their relationship. I was very impressed with her and I knew she would one day be her own brand. She was a single mother with a son that had physical challenges in his youth.*
>
> *Watching her sacrifice her business to take care of her son made her one of my heroes. She showed me what real sacrifice looks like. We developed a high mutual respect for each other. I told her I was going to a hearing for my place in Lawndale. She said her grandfather had an excellent relationship with one of the council members and not to worry.*

Waiting for the final vote was eating away at my skin. I gripped my wife's hand so tight her fingers were turning blue. The last voter was an elderly gentleman who appeared to savor the moment, with the power to make or break me. I looked in the auditorium and saw Chai sitting calmly in the audience. She had a smile on her face like everything was going to be fine. I had to trust it. My stomach was hurting due to my nerves. It felt like the moment when I was on that pitcher's mound. I took a chance and threw the ball. Now we waited to see where the pitch landed. It was out of my control.

I heard a click and saw a green light flash. Everyone celebrated the moment. I do not know if the man who held my vision in the palm of his hand was the man that Chai knew. I did not even care to ask. I was overcome with relief. I also forgot about the money I invested. I had dotted my I's and crossed my T's and now no one could touch me.

I thought about the other gyms. I was concerned that they would get called to the carpet soon. One gym was caught, and eventually had to undergo their hearing. Another stopped operating. I assumed their hearing did not go so well.

To show the slow change of mind for implicit bias: a few years passed and a new fitness facility opened up in the complex across from mine. The manager of the complex walked the new tenants straight over to me to guide them through the permit process. Another gym leasing in the same complex received a warning from the city, and the tenant asked me to guide him through the process. People can see past your pigment when you have the key to their well-being. That is power. Guard it.

All of my seed money was depleted. I hated using corporate credit cards, but if I was to continue, it was time. I got educated on when to use them during my time as a bodyguard.

It doesn't matter how savvy you become at using your influence to get things done. At some point in time, you are going to need a line of credit, a business loan, or to use your credit card. You cannot squander your liquid cash flow. If you do, you will go under fast.

I still needed to market my new place and I wanted to take advantage of the economic specials on billboard and radio spots. Like my father, I did not finish college, and also like him, it was quality people who educated me through life experiences displaying passion, drive and impressive work ethic.

When I was offering personal training at the gym in El Segundo, I also had the privilege of sparring with some of the best grapplers and MMA fighters at the time. It was difficult to focus on training clients all day and miss the opportunity to get the tar kicked out of me by these athletes. I was good enough to be invited to spar with some of these guys and I learned a lot. One day in particular, I was training a doctor. She was in her late 50's but was in phenomenal shape. She had a six-pack and was very toned. She would make 20-year-olds look bad. She wanted to do Brazilian jiu-jitsu calisthenics on the mat, so we did just that.

The fighter of the house, Frank, was on the same mat sparring with a black belt jiu-jitsu instructor. When we finished our mat drills, I overheard the black belt ask the fighter of the house if I knew how to roll or grapple.

Frank nodded his head and said, "A little." Being humble, I did not look directly at them. The black belt said, "Hey, bud you want to roll?"

He had me at hello. We shook hands and began to grapple. We went at it for a little while before he submitted me with a shoulder lock. He actually popped my shoulder out of place. I popped it right back in and continued to roll.

When it was over he said, "You are level-headed, smart, and you don't show ego. Some *brothas* get pissed when they get tapped, but you were super cool. Oh, I heard you were a cop, too."

I did not know how to take that. I was always super mellow when engaging in combative sports, but I knew and had witnessed what he was talking about from others (not that often).

The next day, Frank pulled me aside and gave me a phone number to call a man named Rob. I had no idea why and I did not know who "Rob" was.

When I called, a man answered the phone and said, "Hey CJ, why don't you meet me at the local coffee shop? I'd like to run something by you."

I did not question it. I just went. When I got to the coffee place a sharply-dressed man met me at the door.

"You have to be CJ. I hear you are a pretty decent grappler."

I acknowledged that I was CJ, but replied, "I'm still learning. I just like staying in shape."

We sat down, and he told me he heard about me wrestling the black belt friend of his. He was impressed with how I kept my composure after the session. Out of nowhere, while he was talking, he slightly tipped the table to a point where one of our drinks was falling from the table. I was trying to process why he did that, but the cup had already slid off. I don't know why, but my reflexes fired, and I caught the cup before it hit the ground, while still continuing the conversation.

He appeared assured about me when the cup was returned safely to the table. It was like a weird test. He then said, "Let's get down to business. I provide protection for the best basketball player in the world, and I need diversity on my team. I need an M.J. in the form of a bodyguard."

When he told me who the player was, I was stunned. He told me the pay was not much for home games, but when you travel you make more money. It did not take long for me to accept. This was a once-in-a-lifetime opportunity. Payment was the last thing on my mind. I was going learn or get something else out of this.

The player was revamping his career after a controversial prior year, and I figured the security team really wanted to make sure every member on the detail had their stuff together. I got to travel to places I'd never been. I met people from different parts of the country. I got a bird's-eye view of the player practicing his excellence.

The focus and tenacity of this player was incredible to view. I received mentorship from watching on the side-lines. I would think to myself, *If I could take his energy and apply it to my business, there'd be no stopping me.*

I flew on a private plane and visualized owning the plane for my endeavors. On one flight, I met and sat next to a famous business tycoon, who forecasted how the economy would fluctuate for the next ten years. He was fairly accurate. When I told him the risk I was taking to build my business during a recession, he applauded it. He told me that when everything turned around, people would know where to go. I knew this in my heart—he knew because he had insight.

I never wanted to get close to the star player. When I was with him I did my job and went home, rarely engaging unless he spoke to me. I was a fan, but professionalism was most important to me.

For part of that season, the star was injured. That time was fun for me, because I had more freedom for sight-seeing when traveling with the team.

When he returned, I watched him score 81 points and received an autographed score sheet. I also held the shoes he scored the points in, if that means anything. It was cool at best. I received some of the best training tips from one of the sports therapists on the team. I liked the bodyguard part, but also assuming the role of personal assistant, not so much. I lost my awe of celebrities working in that capacity. I realized they are just people, but that knowledge would help me in the future.

While I worked for the ball player, I was still growing my fitness business, and still had a full-time job working as an officer. I even worked part time as a bouncer at a popular restaurant. I made it no secret from the beginning that my career and business was my priority. I could not schedule myself for many games, and I believe Rob knew that.

One day, he invited me to a popular chicken restaurant. He wanted to share some tips for my business, since I was so passionate about it. He gave me some formulas to create a balanced business plan. One of the more important points that stood out was establishing business credit.

Rob taught me the importance of utilizing credit cards or obtaining business loans at the right moment and why. By the time we were done talking, I lost a layer of fear about using credit cards. I now knew how to make them work for me. I believe this also may have been his way of letting me know that my time was up with the team. I was good with it, because you need to understand how to receive your lessons as an entrepreneur. It was now time to put the lessons learned into action.

Not only did I finally use my credit card, but I also obtained a small business loan. One of my business bankers, Danny, left for a new bank and wanted me to open an account there. He was also a client who believed in my product, and we became friends.

When I discussed my marketing vision, he referred me to the loan department. I met the agent, Debbie, who specialized in business loans. She was an older white woman who was refreshingly nice and took great physical care of herself. She seemed very comfortable with me and it felt like my complexion was not a factor at all. She told me I needed to put together a business plan, and once she approved it we would pursue the loan. I told her I'd have it done in a week. There was only one problem: I had never written a business plan.

The first day of getting the plan together was spent finding business plan software to work with. I forced myself to understand charts, projections and forecasts. I was learning fast and forced to look at my business from an analytical perspective, not just a passion and faith-based approach.

By Friday, the plan was done. I walked it into the bank with a sense of pride. I said to myself, "I did this."

The agent looked over the specs, understanding I was new to this. She looked at me and said, "I'm proud of you. There are some minor items that aren't making sense. I can tell you've never done this before, but for the most part, you've shown you really want this. Let's get this started. First, I'll need to check you and your wife's credit."

> *One of the things I loved about my wife Eva, when I got to know her, more than her looks, was her financial responsibility. When we were dating she wanted nothing from me. She took pride in her independence. What attracted me to her was she did not need a man. If she wanted you, it was her choice. She was the carrot and I was the rabbit. She always had a job; sometimes two. Credit was just as important to her as it was for me. I'm a lucky man. He that has a wise wife truly has a good thing.*

I was a little jealous that my wife's credit score was a few points higher than mine (just like her grades in college). My loan agent, Debbie, an independent woman herself, playfully made sure I knew that. When our loan was approved, she came to my gym to personally tell me. It was a five-year loan, but I promised the agent it would be paid in two years.

Debbie smiled, gave me a hug and before leaving said, "I got a feeling you will. Good luck to you."

My confidence was becoming more like my father's, and in exactly two years I took my daughter Cheyanne with me to pay off the loan. It was something my dad did for me—showing the importance of credit integrity. I was awake during that lesson.

My vision swagger was off the charts after I paid my loan. I immediately purchased a billboard near my gym, and also bought more radio spots for my official grand opening. But when things are going well, people who may appear to support you make some of the strangest comments.

You Have to Run Into a Few Idiots as You Climb

The release of the billboard with my alleged naked body on it drew a lot of attention. I'll admit the billboard was bigger than my gym. It made me feel like I was a big fish, right up there with some of the corporate gyms. In reality, my space was the mom-and-pop storefront of gyms, but I was preparing for the future. Gym managers who saw my billboard walked into my facility and breathed a sigh of relief that I was a private studio. One manager in particular brought his trainers with him. They all looked like steroid freaks from Sweden. They walked in and looked around at how small my place was, then walked out feeling less threatened.

I fed off of that energy. In my mind, they were missing the point. I was not selling a trend or a product—I was offering wellness and life fitness. I'm bigger than four walls.

Business was steady during the recession and I was able to make rent by having independent trainers in my facility who paid monthly rent to me. It made it even easier to pay off those loans. I was in complete control of everything, while the corporate trainer always had to get permission to make decisions. No one was taking a percentage of my profits. I was only beholden to the landlord and the IRS.

About six-months into my new place, I was shopping at the nutrition shop near my gym. While I was at the register, a man walked up to me and said, "You are CJ, right?" I acknowledged.

He then said, "You were my competition."

I replied, "I never knew I had a competitor."

He told me he had to close down his studio because he had trouble marketing due to the recession.

I was surprised, because the economy was beginning to turn around.

He asked, "What did you do to sustain?"

I told him I started marketing and advertising at the worst time of the recession because everything was so cheap. I told him how I was able to negotiate longer advertising contracts. I knew once things turned around, people would know where to find me. It was clear by the look on his face he did not understand. I guess that is why he is out of business.

I did not develop my marketing plan in college. I got it from studying for my first major fitness certification from Aerobics Fitness Association of America (AFAA). One chapter introduced a concept by Dr. John Travis, which discussed the five stages of human behavior.

- The first stage was pre-contemplation. In this stage, clients aren't even thinking about you. In fact, when a friend discusses your business, they tune out of the discussion.
- The next is contemplation: your business is now on their mind. They watch the same friend who mentioned your business changing positively and they may feel there is merit to patronizing you.
- The person then moves to preparation. They may buy workout clothes, go to your site, and check for more references.
- Then they enter the action phase where they test you out to see if they like your product.
- When you give them what they come for, it becomes a relationship of maintenance. It's up to you to continually stimulate the client's interest. This is the relational phase. The client has a trust in you and they provide continuous business through referrals.

It can take months or years to move from the pre-contemplation phase to the action phase. In my case, the time frame of banking on the economy to pick up aligned with the first four stages. When things slightly picked up, along with people hearing the commercials, or constantly seeing a topless muscle-bound man on a daily billboard, I was ready to receive the action. I also made commercials for social media and used those same commercials for cable television spots, knowing you have to constantly put your brand in people's minds.

I continued talking to the man who called himself my former competitor and asked if he would try again. He told me he was not sure. He told me he had quit his job to chase his dream.

I had thought about doing that too, but I'm glad I didn't. Job security is a foundational part of building your dreams.

I put my hand on his shoulder and told him, "If you do start over, you have to think outside the box." I could not quite read the look on his face. But I did not have time to process it. I had a client waiting for me.

Showtime, and other members of my self-defense unit and one supervisor from another unit, who were black, always told me not to be so vocal about my business. They appeared to be protecting me, but slavery was over a hundred years ago, and I was not going to be held captive by fear. The consistent phrase from them was, "They're going to get you, Cleon."

I understood their sentiment, that a person should never promote their business at work. But a person who avoids talking about their endeavors potentially deprives themselves of promotional opportunities. However, you cannot show that your passion supersedes your effort at work. You don't know what your bosses are thinking. You may deserve a promotion, but if you are bragging about your side career, someone may perceive that you may not need that promotion.

It is important to continue seeking growth in all of your career endeavors. You'll get deeper insight for your business. Also, sometimes promotions can be tricky, because focus on them may take away from your passion. You'll have to balance that for yourself.

Your endeavors may also give people above you a reason to pull the rug out from under a work promotion. If you have a side business, you absolutely cannot show fatigue at work. A competing co-worker may use any excuse to put them in the forefront of a superior's mind.

It seemed the few who were not happy with me were the ones always warning me. One of the ways I would identify an acquaintance as an adversary was when I told them I had a business and the first thing that would come out of their mouth was, "Do you have your papers in order?" Those are the people who will most likely cut you if they have the chance, and you should avoid them at all cost.

But your success triggers a positive reaction in some people. This group discovers your passion by surprise or are caught off guard when they hear a commercial, see your gym on a news segment, or hear incredible reviews about your business. They know you are responsible at work and are also respected in your business. It encourages them to inquire about you.

You don't have to throw your success in the faces of other people. Let them discover your brilliance outside of your job. Thank God, I saw that in my father's walk with business.

The strangest comments came when I was accused of false advertisement in the form of a backhanded compliment. Another friend of mine messaged me on social media. He said it was a smart idea to lighten my skin for the billboard to attract white customers. I could not believe what he wrote to me—that was not my intention at all. It was a black-and-white photo. I used that same photo to wrap my SUV.

He may have had a point, because every time I picked up my kids from school, people thought it was the WWE wrestler John Cena on my car. Well, if that brought white customers so be it, and it may explain the look on some clientele's faces when they saw me live and in living color.

I finally notified the gym owner in El Segundo that K-Flash and I were leaving. The owner allowed me to continue teaching the boxing class until one day a student asked if he could train with me privately after class at my studio. I declined. I was honored to teach there, but the student said it within earshot of the owner. I already knew what was coming.

I received a pleasant letter saying my services were not needed anymore. I stopped by the gym to pick up a few things and overheard some of the staff betting that K-Flash and I would be begging to come back in a month. I pretended not to hear that, but it became fuel to prove them wrong. Things were moving for me, but I was not prepared for what was next on the road to the top. "It's showtime."

Surprise!
I'm an MMA Coach?

As a grappler, I used drills from training to get my clients into shape. I had no aspirations of being a real coach in these arenas. I had no time and there was no money in it. I was training three fitness trainers in MMA. Two of them (Julian and Eric) were pivotal in my transition to becoming a fitness trainer. The third was a decent high school wrestler in his day, who just wanted to brush up on his skills for exercise.

We trained for months and the guys got really good. I felt good about the instruction I was giving, because when they went to other grappling schools, they had good sessions there, thanks to my instruction. All I did was take what I learned and show them. It was also a great way for me to stay sharp.

One day while I was sitting at home, Julian called me. He said, "Coach CJ, we're at the gym in El Segundo, and we're going to fight in an MMA match. Can you come down and be in our corner?"

I freaked out and said, "What in the hell are you guys doing?"

Julian replied, "It will be fun. Come on, Coach CJ."

I pondered why he kept calling me a coach.

I was worried sick, so I drove down there to talk them out of it. When I got there, they did not give me a chance to speak.

Eric said, "Come on, Coach. Wrap our hands and let's go over the game plan."

I was nervous because this was where I trained clients and also sparred with the fighters. It would be embarrassing if all these guys got murdered in the ring, because my name was attached. I loved them, and this was the choice they made, so out of a sense of responsibility I assumed the role of coach.

They had the top three fights of the night. Two out of the three won, and the one who lost fought valiantly. It was amazing to hear my clients walk into the ring with the announcer yelling, "From CJ's Functional Fitness."

Here I was, training these guys and they wanted to express what they had learned in an actual fight. I may have been helping them with training, but they helped me with a boost of confidence in what I was teaching them. It only added to my brand.

A few months later, the guys wanted to fight in another match. After the success of the first event I had no reservations this time. When I arrived at the MMA facility, it was nice to see that the crowd remembered my fighters.

I was in the back room getting them ready when one of the fighters introduced me to a gentleman I hadn't worked with before. The young man told me he was fighting, too. I asked if he had any fights and he said he had not. I asked if he ever trained in MMA and the response was the same. Julian asked if I could be in his corner as well.

I immediately told him he should reconsider fighting that day. I did my best to avoid him after that. You could see the young man asking different coaches to wrap his hands, he was denied. It was sad to watch. But he seemed adamant about fighting, so I brought him over to wrap his hands. I told him I was not his coach, but I'd show him some pointers to keep him as safe as possible. He was grateful.

He was the first on the card to fight. I watched him walk onto the mat, seeing him look frustrated that no one was in his corner. I felt horrible; I could not leave him out there by himself. So, I became his corner man. He got his butt kicked thoroughly. In fact, he gave absolutely no competition to his opponent. Thank God, my other fighters won their fights decisively.

One of the house fighters in the gym, a Russian guy nick-named "The Janitor", approached me and asked why I put that guy on the mat with no experience.

My response was, "I did not put him out there. He had no coach. He was determined, and I could not leave him out there alone."

"That explains it. CJ, you are a noble man and I can tell you care about people, but in the fight game, your brand is everything."

I could have been upset with his negative take on the matter, but admittedly, he was giving me useful information beyond the fight world. Plus, whenever we sparred he turned me into a pretzel.

I learned never to put yourself in a position to help someone who is clearly not ready to perform under specific demands in any facet of life. When you see they don't have ability, your job is to tell them they are not ready. If they persist, walk away. You did your part.

If you don't, people will question your judgment, and your brand may take a hit. You won't always get the luxury of explaining your reasoning. One of my worst law enforcement supervisors gave me one of the best quotes I've heard. "Every day is an oral interview." Lesson learned.

First Taste of Prime Time as I Climb

All the advertising appeared to be paying off. My company name was getting out there and people were getting curious about CJ, the man. During a radio campaign, I was able to convince one of the male radio personalities, whom we'll call "K-Smooth," to take some boxing classes. I was looking for an endorsement from one of the talents on the radio station, and he was one of the top disk jockeys at the time. He was known for a deep and smooth voice the female audience loved. His segments were in the noon time slot and he also had a Sunday night faith-based show. I convinced my sales agent, Rochelle, to ask if he would take some classes pro bono, and he agreed.

He showed up to his first class fashionably late. I had no receptionist, so once I got going, my focus was on my class. I was expecting him, so I gave my class a boxing drill and walked outside. Maybe he was lost. When I got outside, he was sitting in his car.

He told me he thought someone was coming to bring him in.

Initially, it came off a little arrogant. I took a deep breath and absorbed that. I told him, "I'm sorry sir, I start my class right on time, but I do understand. Allow me to take you inside."

He saw the energy in the class and immediately jumped in. He saw the focus and intensity of the class, and his air of celebrity disappeared quickly. It was time to work. I went into attack mode, firing up my class. He worked himself into a frenzy and he held his own on the boxing drills. Before he knew it, the workout was over, and he was drenched in sweat. It has been said that the real person comes out during exhaustion in a combative sports work-out. It took a few minutes for him to catch his breath. When he did, a very authentic and warm human being shined through. He engaged with the students and interviewed them about me. The more he visited, the more I liked him, and the students loved his energy.

After he finished his session, he put his voice-over on my new set of commercials with testimonials from the students. It added a personal feel to my commercials, which drew more people. The highlight came when he invited me to his Sunday night show.

I was able to bring some clients and it turned out to be a great show. He told the story of how he came into the studio walking, but crawled out when it was over. He complimented me on the atmosphere of the gym, and the clients I brought to the interview sealed the deal. He never had to prod energy from me, I think that surprised him for a first interview. I was ready. I had my pitch and flow prepared. I was ready for whatever question he and his callers had.

When my clients gave their testimonies, I was able to bring the message home. I added the color commentating about their experiences with me. This was a 20-minute interview that was heading for an hour when a mild earthquake struck and scared him a bit. I don't know whether he had been in California very long. I thought it was funny. It did cut the interview, but I had plenty of time to dazzle the listening audience with my speaking ability. I wanted to show I was not just some cute trainer with muscles. I was talk-show ready, but it took hard work to master the style and flow. I was now on the map—a little bit.

It was important to me that if a media personality was going to speak about my product, they had to experience it first. When you are pushing your brand, you may have to give up some freebies initially. The return of that campaign, monetarily and brand-wise, was satisfactory. I was hoping to develop a deeper business partnership with K-Smooth, but he was moved to the late-night shift. He invited me out to a couple of events: one in particular, a celebrity basketball game. Not to watch, but to play in. Due to work, I could not make it.

The day after the interview, I received many calls from friends and workmates. The running compliment was on how well I spoke. It was no surprise given what I learned from my job. But work was my downside, and there was nothing I could do about it. I missed a couple of opportunities for more face-time with my new radio audience.

> *I had no fear of public speaking. I taught at the academy and pitched for recruitment. My strength was the passion in my speaking. I truly loved speaking off the cuff, leaving caution to the wind. I got a kick out of thinking on my feet and reading audiences. Most of the time I got it right, and when I got it wrong, no one knew. This was one of the things I learned from Showtime. I was good at getting people to focus on the passion, but you get older—that does too.*

> *I left recruitment and took a job in the department as a media relations officer. What I appreciated about that job was that you had to be careful with what you said. You had to be factual or you could potentially ruin the credibility of the agency. You had to develop speaking points for command staff and for yourself. There was a rhythm of speaking when presenting yourself to the media. The pressure was high because one minute you were doing a simple phone interview for a local paper, the next moment you were on a highly-viewed cable news network. There was no room to fail. I also had to perfect my writing ability when producing press releases.*

> *There was a civilian in the media unit I'll call Mr. Frenchy, and his job was to red-line your press release until it was presentable. When he was done, the supervisor would scan through the document and approve it. I thought I was back in first grade all over again. If your spelling was off too many times you'd be in the hot-seat. What I learned from working as a media officer gave the perfect balance to the passionate energy in my business. This is where I improved my writing ability to match the energy of my speaking.*

I learned when to turn on the energy and when to tone it down for effect. I took the position at media because I knew it would strengthen me, and it did. It also allowed me to study excellence in others.

There were two lieutenants I worked under who impacted my growth. J.R. was a workhorse. He was the hardest working person I'd ever seen. His tenacity was brilliant to watch and that is exactly how I learned from him. He was obsessed with ensuring his superiors were happy, I learned how to use that trait later. He spoke softly, to a point you had to shut sound off around you to hear him. Because he had useful information, you did what you had to do to make your surroundings quiet enough to hear him. That was his style. He also had a way of deliberately pausing when asked a question. He wanted you to know he was listening to you. Plus, it kept me on my toes anticipating his answer.

The other was "Cool Andrew." His cool and calm demeanor, even under extreme pressure, was impressive and intimidating, to a degree. When I sparred with fighters, the level-headed ones were the most dominant. My approach came from studying Cool Andrew. Even in his criticism, there was a calm where you focused on being educated rather than fearing discipline.

He got more out of people with that style, including myself. His speaking flow was smooth. When he started speaking, there was a slight nasal growl at first, and then came "the smooth." He closed out each sentence with a faint purr and then a smooth exhale. I believe both were intentional. Studying them helped me focus on my flow. Everyone has a draw in their own way. I embraced my dynamic style, but I adopted some of theirs.

I used all those tools on that Sunday radio interview and showed that I could captivate an audience. My energy, my excitement and dramatic approach forced time to bend a little more for me. This led to more speaking engagements at churches and community centers. Now, instead of speaking off the cuff, I was able to create power points and add themes into my seminars. God was showing me how that was part of the brand, too. It does not matter how attractive you are or how fit you look. People need to be verbally and visually stimulated, and I became very good at providing that.

Your ability to perform on command and sell it is not magic. You have to develop it by perfecting your craft. Even speaking off the cuff is an art form in itself. There is nothing worse than watching a speaker without a plan or credibility. It only takes one moment for a crowd to go sour. Your hands-on experiences build that asset. If someone tells you it is just natural for them, they are lying.

When you master confidence as well as presenting a good message, people will find brilliance in you that most dream to have. People will want to be in your presence because they have no idea what is coming next, but they know it will be exciting.

With all the buzz about CJ's Functional Fitness, things were rolling. I drove home from work one day in slow traffic, due to heavy rain. I had to cancel a client because there was no way I was going to get to the gym in time to train her. Just before full frustration set in, I received a phone call from my pastor. My brother, Deon, told me he would be calling but I did not believe him.

> Deon and Pastor Chaney became really close due to my brother's work in L A.'s downtown skid row. Deon was and still is, one of the top cops in the nation for going above and beyond to serve a population that is often neglected and misunderstood. He took Pastor Chaney on a walk along his beat. As Pastor expressed in a sermon, the residents of skid row flocked to Deon and embraced him, as if he was a prophet himself. I was happy to hear that a new generation of Chaneys and Josephs were becoming friends. Deon put a buzz in the pastor's ear to reach out to me about getting in shape.
>
> The church was growing rapidly. Pastor Chaney's teaching style was elevating his platform to television and radio. I assumed he wanted to be physically ready for the demand, and I appreciated my brother's gesture. Up until then, I rarely tried to make too much contact with the pastor, but I admired him from afar. My life wasn't perfect, so I kept an arm's distance, even when moments opened up to approach my spiritual mentor.
>
> On one occasion, the pastor asked my wife and me to escort him and his wife to the pulpit in the spirit of celebrating their anniversary. My wife and I could not believe they chose us. Our marriage was not in a good place at the time. I guess we hid it well.
>
> I also remember Pastor being near front row during a professional basketball game. I was guarding the star player, and

when he recognized me, he called me by name. I was happy to see him, so I smiled and waved back, but there was no room for any more dialogue. I was comfortable just being proud of his leadership and desired nothing more.

When I answered the phone, I heard, "What's up, CJ? I hear you are doing good, man. Listen—I really need to get in shape. I used to run track and I'm not the athlete I was. It's time. I got to get right."

I had a full client load, but I made room for Pastor Chaney. He was an incredibly focused client, with the exception of his addiction to shrimp. He also practiced fasting for spiritual growth, which went against muscle growth, but he performed well, regardless.

The cutest part about training him was when his wife, the First Lady, Myesha, showed up and encouraged him with Bible scriptures in the middle of an MMA facility. I knew he loved her, because when she showed up, he would go overboard with his kicks and punches to show he could protect her. There was one moment where he was kicking pads, but missed and kicked me instead. Male ego is amazing when it come to the women we love.

Aside from the workouts, I found he was more than just a minister. He was a visionary, and his intensity matched the drive to achieve his goals, whatever goal he set. He too was an "out-of-the-box" thinker and traveled the world to discover how other countries worshiped. It took our growing church a while to catch up with his evolution. He painted a vivid picture of his world education and I wanted to experience the same because of it. Our time together was the perfect mix of conversation and focused training. If he was not a minister, I would still appreciate watching the intensity of his growth, whatever he pursued.

His integrity went way back. I have a special-needs niece he went to high school with, and she always told how kind he was to her when everyone else teased her.

I blushed in church when he referred to his workouts in his sermons. I had a horrible time receiving compliments and expressed that to him.

He told me he had the same issue. I asked him how he handled it, and he said, "Learn to say thank you and move on."

That was therapeutic to me. Sometimes, we make things more complex than they need to be. It takes a lot for someone to hand out a compliment, and to counter it with lack of gratitude, or even worse, to dismiss it by disguising it in the form of humility, is a slight insult.

Pastor Chaney also requested that I train his armor-bearers (security team) in self-defense. I appreciated it, and would have offered my services for free, but he made sure I was paid my worth. That was honorable.

His messages were getting so popular that they gave him a Sunday night slot to run his own show at the Radio Free station. My brother and I were repeat guests on his show. One particular night he was tired and did not have material. I was in the studio making a commercial in the sound room, and when I came out, I saw his look of exhaustion. He was coming in as I was going. He said he did not have a guest and was going to play a recording.

I told him, "You got a guest. I got you. Let's make it a health segment." It was a good show for being off the cuff. Perhaps it was not really off the cuff, since I already had my talking points.

> *With my newfound confidence in public speaking, working as a media relations officer and having a few TV and radio interviews under my belt, I started my own internet radio show called CJ's Functional Fitness Show. I learned how to run a program, with the help of a very special friend named "Big Zoe." He was the program director for the studio. Together, with my small-scale cast, we established a fairly good show that rivaled some radio morning programs.*

It was the beginning of a new venture: internet radio. Our listeners were small in number but engaged. I worked very hard to get guests on the show. First it was willing clients. Sometimes it was trainers in my gym. Eventually we had a few celebrities. Every show had a subject. We had our theme song and I used the commercial I purchased from the radio station I was advertising with to act as fillers in my show. Big Zoe played the role of comic relief. Killer K was the cynical DJ, and the councilwoman played herself. I nicknamed her "The Governor." We even had a frequent wellness guest, a doctor by the name of Natacha Nelson.

Big Zoe was so impressed with my ethic that he broke character on a show and asked to be my client. He lost 72 pounds in a three-month period. With Big Zoe and me, it went from a work relationship to a brotherly bond. With the experience I was acquiring, I was prepared for anything. I just needed the right openings.

As the pastor's show proceeded, I noticed his energy pick up. On an impulse, the pastor created a contest and wanted to pay for the first four listeners who called in to get eight-months training with CJ. I think I surprised the pastor by taking eight people. I offered to take the listeners on at no charge and I'd come back on the show to post results. I had already run a similar campaign years prior that did not start off so well.

In my earliest days of training, we all bore witness to the effects of Hurricane Katrina. I felt sorrow like everyone else, but as a trainer, one scenario I watched on the news gave me purpose. I saw people out of shape and overweight struggling to save their own lives because they were too heavy to pull themselves to rooftops. I saw an interview with a man who lost his wife because he could not pull her out of the water due to her weight. I wanted to help with more than donations. I wanted to team up with other trainers when the storm had passed and offer free fitness training to the people of New Orleans.

The vision was to get the top trainers from across the country to meet and pump them up with a wellness boot camp. I tried really hard to get trainers. I did receive one call from a trainer in Louisiana, but we were never able to connect beyond that one conversation. I needed an avenue to get the word out through the press, so I hired a publicist.

Our initial meeting was at a restaurant. A table was reserved for us and everyone in the place bent over backward for the publicist and her team. They showed us who they worked for in the past, and old news articles. Everything seemed so convincing as she told me of her life struggles and how she recently divorced due to domestic violence. I was sold, but my wife had reservations.

I was upset with her for not believing in my dream. To appease me, my wife went along with it. The publicist's team sold themselves well (against my wife's discernment). Like a fool, I paid more money than I should have for the first installment of their services.

They did press releases and we got some feedback from small publications, but the goal was to attempt to connect with a celebrity to help promote my idea. She claimed she worked for a professional basketball star and would try to make that connection when an opportunity arose. That opportunity came in the form of an auction the athlete was having. The auction would be held at the publicist's home, and there would be some bigwigs and wealthy people at the event. She told my wife and me to dress up.

When we got there, we looked like fish out of water—everyone there was dressed casually. She introduced me as CJ, but kept mentioning that I was a police officer. That was a definite no-no. My wife felt like I was being used. When I asked the publicist if she had pushed my idea, she just told me to go mingle.

There was a news crew there doing a story on the auction. Holding the items would have presented a publicity opportunity, but the publicist got another gentleman who was also dressed nice to do it. Now I understood what my wife felt. She believed I was being used to look like hired security. When another opportunity opened to remind the publicist of our objective, and she interjected and introduced me to her husband, I was confused.

I said, "I thought you were div—," my wife grabbed my hand. She knew I was getting upset. She encouraged me to stay calm and we submerged ourselves in the auction, deciding there had to be a lesson there.

During the auction, there were a couple of items I wanted, but the auctioneer ignored me. After another attempt, the man looked at me and said harshly, "If you want something, you need to speak up!"

With that, I quickly understood the culture. When I left, it was only with a jersey, a poster and a fairly valuable painting signed by the player. It took all I had not to look stupid by turning the place upside down from anger.

Unfortunately, early on, I ended up putting my faith and money in many people who were borderline upstarts or even con-artists. They had backgrounds in entertainment and claimed to have a lot of connections, particularly with the local radio stations. It turned out they had no pull at all. I was able to establish the radio connections eventually, on my own, before letting them go. My ideas went nowhere with them. That is not the way I've seen publicists work for others.

With my bank account empty and a dream defeated, I ended the relationship with that publicist. The experience was embarrassing.

She and others filled me up with what my mother called "pipe dreams." They enticed my vanity and I lost focus on the mission. Instead, I was chasing celebrities. I knew better. I should have listened to my wife. Plus, I was a cop—I was supposed the be the expert at recognizing a scheme.

Sometimes you may get a big idea from God, but you cannot force the issue on your time. Impulsiveness is a silent killer of dreams. I ended up chasing fame more than focusing on the heart of the mission. A few years later, I revisited my idea locally and on a smaller scale. The program was originally called the Fitness Syndicate vs. Obesity. The time was right.

Basically, I was attempting to bring to Louisiana what I would start in L.A. I figured it would cost me nothing to establish on my own, and I'd inherit a wealth of gratitude and self-satisfaction in helping others.

On my word, from the studio interview with the pastor, I trained the eight people and named the event after the pastor's show: Real Life Weight-Loss Challenge. I watched what happens when you give people an opportunity to change (with my gift). One woman in particular, who I called Mama Iris, came to the contest with a severe condition that left her using a walker. I should not have accepted her. She needed a doctor more than a trainer, but I did not have the heart to deny her. She wanted her life back so bad.

By the time the program was finished, she did not need the walker anymore. The other contestants also benefitted, but the true gift was seeing Mama Iris jogging without any assistance.

She gave her testimony on the pastor's show. It propelled my reputation to another level, and I did not have to spend a dime for it. All I had to do was give my time. Two lessons I learned: it does not cost anything to help someone, and to listen to my wife's intuition. I appreciated the fact that Eva never threw the embarrassing moment in my face. She could have, and I would have had to absorb that, shamefully.

The truth is, your wife becomes your passion protector. When we were younger, I considered it nagging when she expressed an opinion different than mine. She knew that once I got spun up on an idea, I took offense to objection. I'd even get upset if she left sticky-note reminders on the refrigerator for marginal tasks.

Reflecting now (in my middle age), I see she was right most of the time. I may not have liked the delivery of her objections, but she was right quite a bit. I now value her opinion and it is paying dividends. I even feel disappointed if there are no sticky tabs on the fridge.

From Man of God to Voice of God

I was in a really good place. For the first time in my life, I was not just a member in the pew. I was part of a church family. The whole vibe of Antioch had changed. Pastor Chaney's teachings were sinking in and you could see the effect the ministry had by the growing diversity in the church. I had no time or desire to become a deacon, usher or choir member, but any time the church needed me, I'd make myself available when called upon.

As long as I've been a Christian, I finally began to understand that God is not a being of vengeance, fire and brimstone as we were taught. God is love, inclusion, patience and kindness. I began to feel comfortable in God's gift of free will to follow the rules or fall off. I understood, most of all, if he wants to use you, he will bring you from a place of darkness or shame beyond man's judgment and understanding.

I'm not attempting to push away my friends who don't believe, but I challenge all to see how, who, and where Christ's interactions with people provide life-changing lessons. Take your politics out of it and just read.

As for me, I found I loved church again and it was my choice. Never again would I let the threat of burning in eternity scare me into slavery or inferiority. The God I understand today, I am in love with. I make my life choices now based on my love for him, not my fear. I am protected when following his rules, I accept the consequences when I don't.

I receive Christ's assurance that there will be no fire for me as promised for those who follow Him— I'll be one mad *brotha* if I discover in the end that I was wrong.

Sitting in front of the church with my family one service, the pastor introduced a guest singer to perform before he taught. His name was Jesse Campbell. He came to the podium, cleared his throat, and belted out the most hauntingly perfect rendition of *Amazing Grace.*

The church was captivated by the perfection of his pitch. I saw gang members crying. I looked at my twin and we both said to each other, "Who is that?"

When Jesse was finished performing, the crowd never recovered. There was almost no need for the pastor to teach.

When the service neared its end, the pastor told me to join him downstairs to meet a friend of his who needed fitness training. Plus, he wanted some men from the church to help set up chairs downstairs, for a meeting the next morning. When I got downstairs, I was led to Jesse Campbell. He was gracious enough to help us set up chairs, and I thought that was honorable. When he spoke, he sounded like the king of pop.

Pastor began sharing his journey with Jesse.

Jesse said, "So you're the dude who's whipping Chaney into shape."

I just laughed.

He continued, "Well, my gut is over my belt. My feet are swollen from all the fried foods I eat on the road. I have dizzy spells, and I've reached the conclusion I need to change."

I gave him my business card and he said he would call me.

I went home immediately and started researching all search engines and social media channels for Jesse. It turned out he had a number one R&B hit in the '90s, which I remembered. I also saw his knock-out performances at championship pro sporting events, singing the national anthem. I researched his gospel concerts and looked up old gospel albums he had. I said to myself, "I got my first official celebrity client." Well, that was not completely true.

> When I first opened up my studio, I signed up a gospel singer. She was extremely overweight and claimed she really needed help, but there was one problem; she was a diva. Her first few sessions consisted of whining and complaining. Just walking ten feet would trigger her to threaten a lawsuit.
>
> In her mind, she could barely walk because of her "broken knees." She tried to intimidate my apprentice at the time, whom we'll refer to as Lady Ann (who happened to be white).

> *Lady Ann was not intimidated. She was from the street. She just had had enough from this diva and did not want to stand in for me anymore. So, I had no back-up for that client.*
>
> *One day, the diva hobbled into the gym, griping as she limped. One of the other trainers turned the radio on, and the number one song in the country was playing. It was an upbeat song that everyone danced to when they heard it.*
>
> *The singer stopped in her tracks and screamed, "Hey, that is my jam!" She began dancing like a high school girl. She jumped and gyrated, squatting to the floor—or as we say in the hood, "Dropping it like it was hot!"*
>
> *I stopped the session immediately. I escorted her out and told her I was not the trainer for her. The look of rejection on her face was priceless, as if no one ever told her no before.*
>
> *I don't need clients bad enough to deal with diva acts, I'm not in awe of anyone.*

Honestly, I did not think I would hear from Jesse again. People say a lot of things they mean in the moment; especially artists.

Sure enough, I was sitting in my office and I received a call—it was him. He was out of town but wanted to set an appointment immediately upon his return. As promised, he showed up and he was on time. I gave the same consult I give all new clients. I got right to business, offering him the utmost professionalism, while being very frank up front as to what my new client could expect from me.

Jesse never flinched. He was serious and wanted to train immediately. He told me he did not have money at the moment because he was working on a project. He promised to pay later, and he did, through tradeouts.

As we continued, he wanted to negotiate a deal where I trained him as his sponsor. So when he performed, he mentioned my company. The deal would expire once his project took off and he would resume paying.

I was a little hesitant, but because he was a reference from the pastor, I figured things would work out. The arrangement worked great. Wherever he performed, he mentioned he was training with CJ of CJ's Functional Fitness.

As we became close friends, he revealed that he was living out of his car while raising his daughter. It was perplexing to me when he disclosed that. With a voice like his, there was no way this was possible, but it was. The entertainment business is not all it seems.

Things were not going well for him. He felt his windows of opportunity were closing. Age was also a factor for him, and music was changing to a point where people did not appreciate singers of his caliber. R&B was taking a back seat to mumble rap and pop music. He basically made his living guest-singing at major churches.

My heart went out to him and I told Jesse I believed in him. I encouraged him to keep singing, but to work on his body transformation. I said to him, "I will continue to sponsor you. I want to see you win. Your physical change will promote change in other aspects."

Jesse worked hard every day. Before he began his routine, he would give a prayer or an affirmation of success. He did not speak in the standard flow of English. He always spoke in poems, mantras and affirmations.

One thing I loved about him: he was approachable to everyone in the gym. He was not the typical "I'm better than you" celebrity type. In the middle of a workout he would break out into song, leaving the gym stunned. It was like having a free concert in the gym. Just a simple note tickled everyone in the gym. He knew how to roll with life. I would throw client appreciation parties and he was never too proud to break out in song. If I needed him at an event, he was there.

God sent another brilliant mind for me to help in Jesse, but he was helping my brand, too. I was associated with excellence. Whenever I needed a video promo, Jesse was right there. He landed a small roll in an inspirational movie produced by a premier televangelist. He received a small jolt of hope and wanted to document his weight loss journey on video, featuring his trainer.

As time progressed, Jesse appeared to look twenty years younger training with me. He was muscular (six-pack included). He shaved his head bald. He kept saying he had something huge coming up, but he could not disclose it. He was so confident with this big news that he finished the video once he reached his goal, before the announcement. The video of his transformation brought thousands of views, but no one was prepared for what was to come next.

Jesse told all of us to tune into one of the major TV stations after the Super Bowl. It was the second season of a major singing competition show called *The Voice*. My family was glued to the television, waiting in anticipation. When he came out and performed, the celebrity judges turned their chairs immediately. He gave one of the best performances of that show to date. Jesse looked amazing! I felt like he was my boxer and I was the coach in his training camp. Jesse was an instant sensation, but in the world of reality television, all of "Team Jesse" got a cold dose of reality.

During his time on the show he was slaying the competition. There were judges bowing to him. While training him, he called one of the judges and wanted her to say hello to me. I was flattered, again. I'm not star-struck but it was a sweet gesture. I said hello and then told him it was time to get back to training. Each week, Jesse put on a Voice performance that humbled even the judges.

One night, Jesse was standing on stage before his coach. It was elimination time and his fate was in the coach's hands. I told my family, "I'm going to bed. We already know Jesse is going to the next round."

As I lay comfortably in my bed, my wife screamed, "Cleon, come down, now!"

I ran down the stairs to the news that Jesse had been eliminated. It felt like someone kicked me dead in the chest, knocking the air out of me. I could only imagine how he felt. In the morning, I woke up in a fog. My soul was crushed. One of the major newspaper articles expressed shock, also.

When I got to the gym, I saw Jesse sitting in the passenger side of his car. His new girlfriend was driving. I was not sure how to approach him, emotionally. So, I waited to check his mood.

He looked up and said, "What's up, man? I feel great, life is good and I'm about to shock the world! This can't hold me!"

I was so impressed with his attitude. He exited the car and told his girlfriend to wait. I immediately started pumping Jesse up, picking up on his momentum. Jesse looked in the gym and saw no one else was there, so he came back to the office and stared at me.

The smile on his face disappeared and tears flowed. Jesse was all man, so when you see a man cry, it hits you hard. He yelled, "How did this happen? What did I do? I've done everything!" He started to slump.

I ran up to him, grabbed him, held him up and hugged him. Forget macho, it was time to be human. I let him cry until someone walked in. I shut the door to the office and made him pull himself together. It must have been how my dad felt when he was making me get back on the pitcher's mound in my youth.

We could not have two grown men crying helplessly, so I made myself the motivator. I told him, "I don't know how, but you will win. Get yourself together, get dressed, it's time to train." The last thing I wanted was for his girlfriend to see him in that state.

Jesse took the momentum from the show and continued to work. He starred in stage plays, had a few movie roles, and toured the world singing. Recently, he returned to train with me again. It had been a couple of years. His intensity was back. I knew something was up.

> *I was driving home from dinner on the freeway, and a song came on the radio called, "Can't Live Without Your Love." They played it over and over again. It was Jesse Campbell. I called him immediately.*
>
> *When he picked up the phone, I told him his song was out and it was hot.*
>
> *He said in the coolest voice, "Hmm, that was supposed to come out tomorrow."*
>
> *Here I was pouring into his life, but he was pouring into mine, as I watched his determination to pursue his dream. I thought, if he can do it, so can I. It began to seep in my soul that passion defeats material desires. When your rocket has not yet launched, you need to spend a little time helping others launch theirs. It will come back to you. I wonder who it was my father helped while in his valley to lift himself. I owe them dinner.*

Reward for Your Effort in the Valley

Whenever I needed my name on the air, the local radio station became my bread and butter. The price to advertise was getting expensive because the economy was turning around, but it paid dividends, so I continued to make myself a household name in the South Bay area.

Rochelle, my sales agent, called me to meet with someone about a community health event hosted by a celebrity TV judge. She told me I had become the go-to guy when it comes to fitness trainers. I had already paid for a set of commercials, so I didn't think it was a sales pitch. She appeared genuine when she said I was ready for the next level. However, the few times she had tried to connect me with new marketing partnerships in the past, had not panned out.

There are no guaranteed connections in business ventures. I learned that from my dad. Everyone is all in with a good idea initially, but people can turn on a dime, especially when the work becomes difficult. This time was different. I had a feeling this was more than me marketing myself—I was about to have my brand attached to my first major event.

I walked into the office and was introduced to a marketing agent representing a major medical insurance firm who was sponsoring the event. I also took a moment to "google" her and discovered she worked with major TV networks. She was the real deal. When I sat down, I was told that they needed a trainer to represent Los Angeles for the nationwide Fit Family Fun Day.

I accepted, and they asked me if I could tie anything into the event. I had experience running weight loss challenges in both my job and business, so I knew immediately what to do to make this event successful.

In the meeting, I suggested that we offer listeners the chance to be entered into a 12-week weight loss program. The conditions were that they had to submit a reason why they deserved to be selected, show up at the event, participate, and twenty people would be selected for a complete fitness makeover. I already had the name for the challenge: The Fitness Syndicate vs.

Obesity. We would select the winners at the Fit Family Fun Day event, after an aggressive radio campaign to draw attention. I was ecstatic, so I added that I could get other local trainers involved to work with the selected participants. The only problem was, the trainers I had in mind did not know it yet.

I invited ten trainers, a doctor, and a husband-and-wife team who ran a Brazilian jiu-jitsu school. Glenn and Jocelyn were my daughter's instructors when she was five years old. I appreciated Jocelyn's energy and patience with my daughter, because Cheyanne was a little chatterbox. Jocelyn had a passion for teaching and I heard she had recently fought through her first bout with cancer. I knew she would inspire the participants with more than her jiu-jitsu. Her journey would give them no excuse to quit, and Glenn's strength in supporting his wife was admirable.

I had to have them on my team. I asked them to meet for dinner at a Cuban restaurant in Manhattan Beach. I told them what it was about, and they immediately accepted.

The trainers at my gym agreed to meet for discussion at a luncheon. My friends K-Flash, Henry, Jon, Julian, Eric, Big Sean, and Chai all said they would help. A local doctor also joined us at the restaurant. I invited my old grappling instructor and former MMA Champion, GI Joe Charles. The luncheon looked like the who's who of personal fitness training. I made my pitch as to what I was planning to do, using a PowerPoint presentation, and everyone bought in except the doctor. She seemed scared to participate, but I understood, with her profession and the liability issues that come with it. Most of the group agreed on my name alone.

> *I remember when my father and mother were barely pulling themselves out of financial crisis. My dad called and wanted me to come to an investor's meeting. I did not want to hurt his feelings, but I was not about to invest in anything. The economy was too risky. I went to the meeting just to show face. My father had gathered local property investors (most he knew) to pool*

together to form an investment group. Everyone in the room understood his current state of affairs, but they did not care. He rented an office space for the evening, because at the time my parents had left their five-bedroom house and moved into a trailer home. The room was full of men who were familiar with his legend. Historically, they knew that when he had an idea, you did not ask, you just got behind him. Almost everyone bought in, but I was just not ready.

At the time, I had a job as a police officer and it was no time for risk. But sitting in that room, I was blown away by people who believed in Dad, especially in that moment in his life. It was a common place when he was on top of his game, but this was different. These were also people he had trained and mentored to become successful. They all had the same entrepreneurial twinkle in their eyes that he had. I could not relate because fear of losing held me back (from what I witnessed in the past), it repressed that twinkle in my own eyes.

I had missed the lesson back then, but the code was wired inside of me to create the same influence. Dad passed on more than good looks. He passed on the success gene and it was coming out. Watching Dad conduct that meeting, I began redefining what success really is.

It is nice to have a physical savings account, but you need what I call the connection savings account. You need to build that account with people you have helped before. You let them sit in that account and it draws interest until you need it. This is the type of account you cannot expect to draw out of as you desire. It's there waiting, when your life hits distress.

By the end of my dinner, everyone was excited about the program and all trainers were on deck. The radio promotion was a success and we received hundreds of social media and text inquiries about being selected to my program. Rochelle asked if I could wrap my truck with an ad to draw attention at the entrance of the event. That is when my basic SUV became "The CJ Mobile."

During the initial walkthrough of the mall where the event would be held, the radio station production team, the marketing agent, insurance sponsor and mall security met with me, along with my wife and my trainee, a former homeless woman named Lady Ann, whom I was mentoring to be a fitness trainer. I helped her while she was piecing her life back together. She was a great asset to me while she was growing.

In my mind I thought, *I was just the talent. Why do I need to stay for the whole walkthrough?*

What my wife and I discovered was they were leaning on me to plan the flow of the event. I had no idea I was going to be the main focal point. I thought I was just going to pump up the crowd and make the selection of the participants for the program. I was the show. I was shocked, but I was ready.

Rochelle looked at me and said, "I told you. It is your time."

I reflected on my season as a physical training instructor, a recruiter and a media relations officer. Recalling what I had done in the past in preparation for this moment, it was easy to accept my role as the go-to guy.

The event was an absolute success. The mall was packed. The radio station street team of DJ's was engaged throughout the entire event. I kept the crowd energized with a walk around the mall, which my daughters helped lead. My oldest, Cheyanne, helped me bark commands, and my youngest, Zaire, wiped sweat from my brow as I got worked up leading the crowd on an intense boxing aerobic session.

One of the main disc jockeys, Nautica, embraced the energy and kept the flow at a high pace on air, as did a TV personality. It was now time to announce the selectees for my fitness program. The final two would be people in the audience who showed the most energy during the workout.

I brought all of the trainers on stage. I could see they knew I was onto something. The jiu-jitsu couple mentioned to me (on the side) that I needed to turn this into a TV documentary or reality series. I was flattered but I was not thinking that far yet. To see the selectees cheering, crying and hugging each other as if they had won the lottery was an indescribable feeling of joy to me. We were about to save people's lives, and my once failed vision to help a mass of people was now revived. The names were also confirmed over the radio for effect. My pastor showed up towards the end of the event, which meant a lot to me.

My presentation went so well that a convenience store chain representative, also a sponsor of the event, wanted to discuss using me as a health ambassador in a potential marketing campaign. The marketing agent representing the insurance company overheard the conversation and wanted to be a part of the negotiation. I looked to my wife and naively said, "I think we've made it." I had visions of leaving my job, and I almost did, until another dose of reality hit.

The average weight loss during the Fitness Syndicate vs. Obesity program was twenty-two pounds. We exposed the participants to every fitness trend possible. The winner lost thirty pounds. It was such a success that the following year, a news outlet covered the event.

The year after, the American Heart Association attached themselves to my program, and the winner that year lost fifty pounds.

The Fit Family Fun Day event was a success, and with all the attention received, I knew we were on our way to fame and fortune. But I had to learn yet another harsh lesson.

I was looking for a person to bring me out into the public eye. I figured all I needed was this event. Sadly, I was mistaken.

Ego is One Hell of a Drug When Climbing

My wife and I learned that the marketing agent wasn't exactly as she represented herself. She seemed to be in the business of making a profit from connecting businesses together for promotional campaigns. She expressed full confidence that my brand was marketable and told us she could tie us in with a convenience store chain for their campaigns, which would benefit all of us.

My wife and I had a card from the convenience store rep and could have called directly, but we did not have experience in negotiating contracts of this nature, so we put our faith in the marketing agent. She had experience in the field and her credibility, from what I researched, made us feel confident she could walk us into a deal faster than we could ourselves. I was taken aback by how impressed she was with us.

We appreciated the insight she gave us on how to navigate this level of business. If she could connect my brand with a national chain, the sky was the limit. Unlike the publicist I'd dealt with earlier, this woman knew what she was doing. The only concern I had was that I believed she over-quoted our side of the offer to work with the company. But it seemed to make sense. The higher the agreed upon fee, the higher percentage she got from the deal. But I still thought the quote was a little high for a first time marketing collaboration. But it seemed there was no bargaining down.

I called occasionally to see where we were at with the deal, during the first few weeks. The last call came with a chilling dose of reality. The agent told us the company was not biting. I inquired (for educational purposes) as to what went wrong and where we needed to move from there. After a moment of silence, she simply replied, "Well guys, on to the next one."

I did not understand what she meant. I figured we were going to find another chain to work with.

But my wife was also on the phone and got the message immediately. She put her hand on my shoulder, kindly thanked the agent, and ended the phone conversation.

I looked at my wife, confused.

Eva said, "She's done with us. It's a wrap."

That was when the cold-hearted truth hit me. I replayed the last seven words the agent said in my head at a slower speed. My heart dropped, the vision I had of leaving my job as a police officer was painfully erased.

I was not mad at the agent. She was the most honest person I'd dealt with, even when letting me down in my quest for brand recognition. She did not string me along. She gave it to me hard and fast. It hurt just as much that way, but the ability to move on and regroup faster proved a positive.

I kept myself busy, getting back to small speaking engagements to stay sharp and relevant in the community. I had a tough letdown, but I knew it was not over. I just needed to keep pushing. I was good enough to be approached once and it would happen again.

What I learned was that life outside of a secure job is unpredictable. You don't just up and quit your day job. You have to learn to use your steady employment as the fallback to keep you sustained when your entrepreneurial ideas fall through. Your employment is your constant. That would be affirmed again, later.

Be a Mentor, Not a Savior – Not Worth Your Marriage

While working in my gym office, I received a phone call. I heard a woman's voice on the phone. "I've been looking at your website. I like the fact that you teach Functional Fitness, but you really dive into the spiritual side of wellness."

I truly appreciated her recognition of that. It was my first introduction to Lady Ann. She said she did not want to be a client. She told me she was having a difficult time getting into corporate gyms and felt she was lacking experience. She was unemployed, so she had all the time in the world to learn.

I felt comfortable with her and told her if she wanted to come to the gym, I would help her with whatever she was weak in. I said, "Be at the gym tomorrow at 5 a.m. for your first lesson. In three months, you will be ready."

She was not late, she absorbed the lessons well, and everything was going fine. She asked if there was something she could do for me.

I said, "Someone trained me like I am training you. I'm paying it forward."

Lady Ann, out of gratitude, would clean the gym, organize my files and substitute train for my private clients and boot camp classes. She helped me with media campaigns and even ran errands for me. I thought it was great. I could take breaks, spend time with my family or promote my business with the free time I had.

The three-month lesson turned into a year; and on top of that, I got her in the best shape of her life.

I gave Lady Ann a few clients, so she could make some money for herself. I did not feel comfortable with the barter system anymore, plus she had learned enough to be trusted with my brand. The longer she stuck around, the more I got to know her background. It turned out that her life was full of tragedy. She had been through life's ringer and it showed on her, physically.

It felt great that she would confide her life story to me and I was glad my gym could provide a place of relief for her. I believe that became the problem.

Lady Ann spent all day at the gym, to a point where, in my perception, she established a stake in it. One day, she got testy with a group-class client. When I spoke to her about it, she became upset that I did not take her side.

She said to me, "This is my house!"

I replied, "No, this is not the streets. This is my business, and it is important that the customers are happy." At the time, I hadn't picked up on the signs that I was becoming a savior for her.

The biggest problem involved my wife. Lady Ann would rarely address her, and the feeling was mutual with Eva. I told you my wife is a very passive-aggressive person. My wife spoke her mind about concerns at what felt like the oddest times to me, but she took a few days to process things before she expressed them verbally.

Fed up, Eva finally told me, "Lady Ann does not speak to me when I come to the gym. And what's more insulting, she treats our children as if they are hers."

I did not see it that way, but I promised I'd talk to Lady Ann about it. When I brought up the issue to Lady Ann, she became irate.

She said, "She does not talk to me. Besides, she does not even come in here. I do what she should be doing. I know you are frustrated about it, too."

She was right about my feelings, but I realized she came from the perspective of a single woman with no children. As my wife had pointed out, Lady Ann had no responsibilities and all the time in the world.

At that time, Eva and I were working through another challenging period in our marriage. I was frustrated that she had no time to help promote my business, and she was frustrated I was not home enough with the family helping with our children. We were both navigating against what, in our minds, a perfect partnership should look like.

This argument is not new to couples. As a husband, I felt I had a job and a business to look after. My wife had a job and took care of our young kids. Both of us wanted to be understood.

Lady Ann picked up on our issues, especially after I vocalized my frustrations to her just to get them off my chest. The situation was out of bounds.

Things began to get more uncomfortable when I took on a new client, an elderly woman I was assessing. Lady Ann shadowed me.

Shadowing is when the trainee watches and assists the instructor. I introduced Lady Ann to the client as my apprentice. I went to the bathroom and left Lady Ann with the client. When I returned from the restroom, I could tell something was off. The appointment ended abruptly, and I wondered why. It left me confused.

During my phone consult with the woman prior to the appointment, I had bragged about my wife, kids, and family environment in the gym. The woman commented that it was one of the things that drew her to my business. She heard I was a great trainer, but she also heard I was a loving husband and father.

I normally do not follow up with clients after an initial assessment. I believe that if I cannot close the deal, then I am not meant to have that client. I want to be sure about choosing a client and I want my clients to be definitive about choosing me.

But in this case, something inside told me to call the woman. When I did, she told me she did not want to be a part of any mess. She told me Lady Ann said she wished I was divorced. I was startled by that. I admired Lady Ann because she was a great student, but hearing this made me uncomfortable and angry. I was proud of my professionalism. I'd heard horror stories of other gyms closing down over this kind of foolishness.

A few other clients also approached me and shared their concerns that having Lady Ann around all day gave the impression that something was going on. Another trainer told me she had gone to a pub with Lady Ann, who disclosed some unsettling things about her feelings. The trainer made it clear to Lady Ann that Eva and I were like family to her, and not to push those boundaries with whatever she felt toward me.

I began seeing what my wife was feeling. It became even clearer when Lady Ann called me at 1 a.m. one morning. She woke me up and told me she was stranded near her apartment and wanted me to pick her up. I calmly told her to call a tow-truck. It was as if my wife did not even exist in her mind.

The final confirmation came when I went into the gym one morning about 5 a.m. I unlocked the door and heard the sound of a treadmill. No big deal—other trainers used the facility. I opened the office door and there was Lady Ann on the treadmill, but her outfit did not look like it was geared for training. It looked like she was wearing a two-piece bathing suit. I was stunned. The look on my face must have given it away.

She looked at me and said, "It's okay, I feel comfortable like this only around you."

I literally walked backwards out of the office and out of the gym.

I went home immediately and did some deep breathing until I could calm my nerves. Eva had already left the house to drop off the kids and head for work. I felt so uneasy I stayed home all day until Eva got back home. I could not share what happened that morning, but I did tell Eva it was time for Lady Ann to go. If you ask Eva, she'll tell you that she demanded Lady Ann leave. Either way, she had to go.

I told Lady Ann, "I really appreciate all you've done here at the gym, but the buck stops with my wife. Eva may not show up here often, but whenever she decides, it is her right to. She has her own job and manages the children."

I completely avoided discussing the issue of that morning.

Lady Ann did not argue, she just said, "I'm moving back up north. There is nothing for me out here."

The day Lady Ann left, she stopped by the gym to say her goodbyes to all the trainers. She thanked me for everything and I gave her a hug. My wife happened to arrive to pick up the kids at the gym at that time. The kids ran up to Lady Ann and gave her a big hug. As soon as Eva saw Lady Ann leave the gym, she got out of her car, waltzed into the gym with the biggest smile on her face.

Eva will tell you that Lady Ann left when she parked and jumped out of the car to "clean house." My wife's version was probably the right one. Either way, Lady Ann left and that was the day Eva assumed her place as Mrs. CJ of CJ's Functional Fitness.

Eva showed her mean streak and I thought it was sexy. It started a turnaround for our relationship. Her presence in the gym was a strong factor in client growth and attraction. My clients loved our interactions together. It gave them a stronger sense of trust in my brand because the whole family was actively involved.

Eva began showing up more regularly as our children became less dependent. Eventually, she became a certified trainer, and helped me out with classes and events. That was a blessing. Maybe that was a wake-up call for her, too. I don't think Eva worried about me "crossing the line." But she did not want another woman attaching to me.

I was responsible for how things went down with Lady Ann. I should have stuck to my boundaries. When you go from mentor to a knight in shining armor, that is a slippery slope. For weaker men or women, it is easy to fall into traps.

The perception looked bad with Lady Ann. Some clients and a few associate trainers would subtly let me know. I was guilty of being naive, but not of violating God's rules within my assignment. I feared that the most.

Since Lady Ann's departure, I've mastered my mentoring skills. When it comes to mentoring new entrepreneurs today, I keep the time window of that relationship short. If I cannot get them up to par within a certain period of time, I have to end the lesson. If they get their certification and want to grow their business out of my gym, they pay rent immediately. Most importantly, they get to know Eva, the queen of our castle.

When a mentor conducts himself or herself with accountability, there is a healthier professional etiquette. The friendship grows as the professionalism increases. I tell young entrepreneurs to this day, that a major part of success is keeping your brain in your head, your heart in your chest, and your private parts in your pants.

There comes a point in time where you have to stop calling on your gurus or mentors. I used to call Mr. Evans chronically for advice, when things were not going right or when I needed a brilliant pep talk. That clearly should not have been his constant role in my life. When mentors give you advice, the next conversation should be about positioning a move up. They cannot help you when you keep bringing the same problems to them. When they offer suggestions from their expertise, it is not a motivational session, but a subtle instruction. I've learned, do not treat your mentor like the church: save your repeated "laying of your problem at the altar" for Sunday service.

There is nothing worse than when you call your mentor on the phone and he or she won't pick up. If it happens repeatedly, they aren't busy, you are becoming an energy-zapper. It is not that they don't want to talk to you, they just need to build up energy for what you may bring. When you get instruction from a mentor, it comes from experience. Their experiences may not be exactly like what you're going through, but the formula to better yourself is the same. They see things about your situation before you do because of their insight.

Do not waste their time calling with the same thing or debating their recommendations. Remember, you chose them. If you disagree, stay quiet and move on. I had to force myself to call only when I had elevated from the advice given. Mentors are waiting to pour more into you, but you have to listen. Beyond that, keep it to friendly conversations.

I could not share this with you until I became a mentor for others. One woman, who was in the beauty industry brought these insights home.

She was a fitness client at first, but as time progressed she disclosed that, like me, she had a full-time job and a new business venture. I walked her through my journey, sharing how I navigated my business. Like mine, her business was considered a luxury item.

Of all the advice I gave, she never attempted the one thing I recommended to put her on the map locally: radio advertisement. I gave her my sales contacts. I called my sales agent to let her know she may have a new client. Rochelle and the lady even had a few meetings and became friends. But three months passed, and the client came into my office, depressed. She felt like all hope was gone and her business was not moving anywhere.

I asked her one question, "Did you ever advertise with the radio station?"

She gave me every excuse but the answer I was looking for.

I told her I could not help if she did not at least make the effort. Then I changed the subject to address other issues in her life. She was a good friend, but I could only give advice where I could help. She eventually stepped up to the plate.

Another example comes from a gentleman I mentored, someone I consider a friend—in some regard, close to a brother. I don't mind being in his presence outside of mentoring, but after all the advice I gave him, he is still doing the same hustle, but in a different way.

This man refused to get licenses and certifications in his field, which would have put him in position to obtain high-profile clients. Your certifications, licenses, and insurance let your potential clients know you've worked to become legitimate. It shows you are responsible and accountable.

This man is extremely talented, but if it is not an easy hustle, if payment is not cash upon delivery, he wants nothing to do with it. He doesn't realize that just because the hustle changes, does not mean the hustling stops. Some people are hustling fools. If they are friends, love them where they are. If not, drop them immediately or you'll waste energy.

If you assume the role of mentor, put a time limit on it. When time expires and no results are shown, move on or your mentees' disease of mediocrity will infect you.

Secrecy Cannot Hold Excellence

I was at my gym listening to the radio station I advertised with when I heard the early morning personality, Adai Lamar, mention my name during her show. She was talking about my DVD cover, telling the female listeners how muscular my body was.

I chuckled, because I didn't think she remembered when I came to the studio a couple of years prior as a recruiter for my department, wearing my uniform. She was kind with a down-to-earth hospitality, when she walked me into the studio. To see her in person giving traffic updates was worth studying. Her enunciation was impeccable. When it came to my business, I really appreciated how she promoted my spots.

My sales agent, Rochelle, told me that another radio personality wanted to train with me, but I had no idea who, and I did not need to promote anything new. My plate was full.

A few weeks went by, then I received a phone call at the office from what sounded like a secretary. She said, "CJ, Miss Adai Lamar would like to set an appointment with you."

"Sure," I said.

She came to the studio and sat down for the consultation. I did the standard body fat, weight, and goal assessments, but I also wanted to set the tone that I was a professional. I told her, "I have no time for games. I'm married, and I take my job seriously."

This is something I tell all potential clients. It puts those at ease who are serious, and wards off those with different intentions. She told me she had a fitness coach before, but due to her new schedule she could not get to him. We all knew who her coach was.

> *Coach E was (and still is) a legendary mainstay at the station. New trainers like myself considered him a fitness guru. Every*

Wednesday he gave motivational and spiritual fitness tips. He was a juggernaut when it came to community work.

I was the new kid and I highly admired him. I met him in person once while I was on the rise. I was told to go to a news telecast promoting the station's annual KJLH's Women's Health Forum, a very popular event sponsored by the station and local businesses. I walked into the broadcast area, a sea of black T-shirts with the coach's logo, wearing my white CJ's Functional Fitness T-shirt and hat. Even the news reporter looked at me like I was not supposed to be there. I was embarrassed, but Coach E went out of his way to meet me personally and give well wishes on my career. He was as gracious in person as he was on the radio.

When it came to Adai, this was not a client take-away from Coach E, but a circumstance of opportunity. I perceived this moment as honoring the coach with my best. I knew taking on a client like Adai, who already worked with the best, would require excellence from me at all times.

The assessment was going well. She was very honest with herself. She knew she was overweight due to personal life struggles, which is common for many women dealing with stress.

I thought, *If I can get her in shape, then my brand will be solidified.* There was just one problem.

She said, "I do not want anyone knowing I have a trainer, and I do not want anyone to know my name in your gym."

Being realistic, I thought, *Okay, this is not going to help the brand at all, but she will still get my best.* I told her I would give her a different name in the gym.

Instead of Adai Lamar, I called her *"Adrianne Leonard"* or *"A.L."*

She chuckled and said, "Perfect!"

We started training immediately. I would call her Adrianne, and it would take her a minute to respond. I got a kick out of seeing that.

She wanted to learn boxing to shock her into shape, and I accommodated that, initially. After all, I had a boxing DVD that inspired her to seek me out. I saw much more potential in her fitness ability. I decided to sneak in the full spectrum of functional training, MMA-style. I trained her like a fighter and she was all in.

There were funny moments because she was super analytical. She questioned everything, and I answered whatever she threw my way. She brought out the best in me because I had to dig deep to educate a client who was not trained in functional fitness.

She became a mentor in the form of a sister. She educated me on how she navigated her field of entertainment. I was learning how not to be so rigid and anxious with time and structure. I realized life is not like the police department, not black and white. You have to be able to navigate through gray.

In a couple of months, Adai had lost over thirty pounds. She also ended up with an overall body fat of 17% (well under the standard for women, which was 25%). It was one of my greatest successes—but no one could know about it. However, I had gained an adopted sister. But a surprise was on the way.

I was driving to work, listening to the morning show, when I heard Adai talking about a secret she was going to disclose at the end of the week. She advised listeners to stay tuned.

Friday came, and during her segment she began to discuss her struggles and her weight gain because of the stress of taking care of her mother. By that time, many people had noticed her amazing weight loss over such a short period of time. Some thought she was on a new weight loss product from one of the other advertisers. Then she unleashed her secret. She told everyone listening about the amazing CJ of CJ's Functional Fitness.

Her morning show had become nationally syndicated. Her testimony was bigger than any billboard or commercial I ever put out. My website blew up and I became highly visible on web search engines. Even my old stuff was popping up. My social media pages boosted faster than ever. She even brought me on the show. The response was incredible. I was no longer a rising name in the fitness game—I *was* the game.

The visions of quitting my day job resurfaced in my head. I did not need many private clients because my group classes were overflowing. Women empowerment groups were ordering classes, women's motorcycle clubs were coming my way, and big community events asked me to host. The best part for me was no longer having to lie to my wife about my client's name.

It was now time to unveil CJ to the world. We just needed a proper event for the unveiling.

A Vitamin B Shot Before Launch

I had a moment of doubt in the middle of my good fortune. You might call me a positive pessimist. It means I'd rather think of the worst-case scenario, so if something does not go well, my emotions remain balanced.

I was training a client by the name of Glenda Greene. I called her "Sergeant Greene" because of her commanding presence and self-discipline as an entrepreneur. She too, had my dad's swagger. She was a life insurance agent referred to me by Adai.

We hit it off immediately and became instant friends. I loved her ability to get on the grind and hustle for herself. She became my insurance agent when she got me to understand the importance of leaving a legacy for my family, with simple common-sense pitches.

The one thing that sold me was when she said, "CJ, after you die, how much is your family worth to you?" I bought life insurance immediately.

One week in particular, I was griping about not being able to grow my business full-time. By our final workout for the week, she had had enough.

She grabbed me by the shoulders, pinned me against the wall and said, "CJ, if you are going to quit your job, then do it. You are CJ and you got what it takes to be successful. Quit being a punk a**, make your decision, and deal with it! I believe in you! Do you?"

I swear, I almost called work and quit that day. Glenda Greene was the female version of my father.

Like many black kids raised in the '70s, I developed an inferiority complex. Everything good, smart and beautiful on television was white. Everything bad, ugly and stupid was black. Our motivational movie was Roots, a slave movie, and the only television show where anyone had anything was The Jeffersons. There were two other shows we all enjoyed, but the entertainment industry made sure we knew where our acceptable place was in society: *Good Times* and *Sanford and Son.*

I remember my mom and dad agreeing to bus us to a mostly white junior high school. It was rough because there were enough hostile white kids to create the perception that black students were not wanted. I did not quite fit in with the black kids because I had good grades and good citizenship. I was a nerd and my nickname in school was Gumby. My brother was not a nerd, but he inherited Gumby II. I was accused of wanting to be white. I was a loner, for the most part. My dad got tired of me walking in the house with my head down. He had enough of me crying in my mother's arms about how lonely I was.

One night, I was in the kitchen washing dishes. Dad got up and began sleepwalking right to the refrigerator. That was not uncommon for him. He guzzled down a whole milk carton. Then he began smashing roaches he saw on the counter.

I just laughed in amusement.

But that night, he stubbed his toe and it woke him from his trance. He said to me, "Hey Cle-Cle," that was my nickname.

With my head down, I said in a low-pitched voice, "Hey." That did not set well with him.

He turned me around and said, "Look at me, boy. Look me dead in the eyes and don't take your eyes off mine."

I had no idea what I did, but I did not take my eyes off him.

He continued, "What is your last name?"

I meekly said, "Joseph."

He said again, "Boy, what is your last name, and you better say it like you mean it!"

I said as loud as I could, "Joseph! Dad, I am Cleon Joseph!"

Dad released my shoulders, stepped back and said, "You d*** right, young man! Start acting like it. You are just as good as anyone."

With the success and promotion spurred by Adai Lamar, and the push from Glenda Greene, thoughts of quitting my day job ran through my head. Thank God, my wife painted our whole financial picture and stopped me.

Eva has always provided the balance to my impulsive nature. But I'll never forget that shot in the arm from *Sergeant Greene*. Maybe I'll utilize her advice wisely in the future.

Los Angeles, We Have Lift-Off

I was invited to kick off the Radio Free station's annual KJLH Women's Health Forum at the Los Angeles Convention Center. It had grown into a major event, drawing thousands of women looking for information on health and wellness, and thousands of men checking out the women. The year prior, I was asked to do a brief warm-up and run a vendor booth. This year, I was being unveiled as a headliner.

The first part of the morning, I started off warming up the crowd with a boxing aerobic workout that I had choreographed. I wanted to make sure I was on fire when I came out. Adai set up the anticipation for my introduction.

Earlier, she made a social media video of her journey with me. It added more coals to the fire for the build-up. That day, Adai reminded people of her own journey to fitness, as she had over the radio. Her energy sent the crowd into a festive fervor. I was just as anxious as the crowd.

Finally, she unleashed *the beast*. "Ladies, get ready to be pumped up by my trainer, CJ of CJ's Functional Fitness!"

I grabbed the mic like a hip-hop star with his first platinum hit. I had a form-fitting red shirt that showed every muscle on my body. I started yelling, "What's up, Radio Free Family!"

The crowd went nuts. The women were screaming as if M.J. hit the building.

I picked up the energy and felt outside of myself, "God is good."

The crowd responded. "All the time!"

I repeated, "God is good."

Almost 4000 women screamed louder, "All the time!"

I knew I had the crowd in the palm of my hand, so I threw them a curve ball with the next run. I yelled, "And God wants us to work out!"

They screamed, "All the time!" Then they all caught the joke and there was a mass of contagious laughter.

That kind of control over a crowd was indescribable.

I had picked upbeat music that was very popular. It did not matter the age or health of the audience, everyone worked out at my command.

When it was over, I was drenched in sweat. I felt like the Godfather of Soul—all I needed was someone to bring my cape. It was my "drop the mic" moment.

The crowd was in a frenzy and it was difficult for Adai to the bring the energy down to start the panel discussion. The commotion bled into the live telecast, which made the anticipation for the discussion that much more enticing for me as a guest panelist.

I changed out of the skin-tight outfit and into my company T-shirt just before the panel discussion. I was still processing what had just happened. The other panelists, comprised of doctors and celebrities, gave me high-fives.

Adai walked up to the stage and whispered, "You ready, my brother?"

I just gave a wink, smile and a nod. When my turn came to speak, women demanded that I show my six-pack, and I did. The crowd lost control, while Adai did her best to calm everyone back down.

I finally spoke about the spirituality behind functional fitness. Before I could get into the meat and potatoes of my lecture, a congresswoman interrupted my presentation to discuss the Affordable Health Care Act, and a political party's resistance to the bill. I was angry that I had been cut off, but I realized there was more of CJ to take in throughout the day.

The radio station had big plans for CJ and Adai. They asked me to do another warm-up with another radio personality for the next panel discussion.

I knocked it out of the park and moved to the next phase of the day—a fashion review to give the ladies some more eye candy, hosted by Adai.

Adai had asked if I wanted to be a part of the show and I agreed to it. She wanted to give the crowd another hit of her trainer, CJ. I went backstage to find some clothes. I watched all the male models practicing their struts, spins and turns. I was a little intimidated, because these guys were smooth.

The models grabbed all the best robes and furs and briefs. I was left with a pair of colored shorts from a local convenience store, and a snorkel. The other guys primped and fluffed, adjusting their underwear so they looked just right for the ladies.

One model walked up to me and asked if I would look him over to see if he was *fluffy* enough in his mid-region.

Standing in my pair of discount shorts and snorkel, I calmly said, "You are good, bro. Now, please close up your fur coat and save it for the stage."

The models decided I should go last, because I had the least experience. Translation: they did not want me to ruin their show. I watched and heard the ladies work themselves up, but the energy was not quite what it had been earlier that morning. Each time a model came offstage, they were congratulated by other members of the troupe.

My turn came, and Adai prepped the crowd. I peeped from behind the curtain as she mentioned my name. I saw every woman in the building surge up to the stage. Adai said, "Ladies, you got a taste this morning. Now coming to the stage, making a guest appearance on the catwalk, my trainer—CJ, of CJ's Functional Fitness!"

I took a deep breath, threw my snorkel on the ground and stepped out. It was complete pandemonium.

With every step I took, the crowd wanted more. I told myself, *I am not a model. I am a trainer. I'm going to do my thing.*

I dropped to the floor of the catwalk and performed push-ups and bear crawls. Women were grabbing my legs and pants. Some were climbing on stage. You could hear Adai doing her best to regain control of the crowd. I heard and felt the catwalk bending under the weight of the women. I got to the end of the catwalk and stood up triumphantly, stretching out my arms. I felt like the most electrifying force in the building.

My wife was in the back, working our information booth with her mouth wide open. She did not take the pawing women too seriously, she was used to that, though this was different.

A woman standing next to her and my daughter yelled, "I just want to take CJ home and whip him. I wonder if that sexy man is married!"

My wife replied in her mild manner, "Yes, he is married to me."

She finally understood the magnitude of my being.

> *I met Eva Nicole Khan on the first day of college at California State University of Long Beach. I had no plans for a girlfriend—I wanted multiple girlfriends.*
>
> *My high school sweetheart had moved to Texas with her family. I don't think we officially broke up, she just had to leave. I was non-committed, and with all the beautiful young women in college, I planned to make the most of it. That all changed on a Tuesday during Black Studies class. As soon as I sat down at the round table of Dr. M's class, I saw Eva and we locked eyes. She looked like a cute chipmunk. She had strong Caribbean features, thick lips, and a nose like I had never seen on a wom-*

an before. I had no doubt I was going to approach her, but I needed a way in.

Dr. M was a very stern teacher from South Africa. He loved black people but was very hard on American blacks. I think his intent was to help us understand that we did not know what real struggle and sacrifice were about, compared to Africans from the Continent. There, they value education despite harsh adversity. Dr. M felt American blacks did not value their opportunities, especially black men. He would even tell the men in the class that they were not worthy of his daughters.

With each class, he drove that message home. He had this habit of getting so spun up on his soapbox that white spittle formed at the corners of his mouth. I got a kick out of him walking around the class, standing behind individual students. I had hilarious visions of him standing over those who were not performing well in his class, until the spittle fell on top of their heads.

I was able to non-verbally direct Eva's attention to the teacher's mouth. It was funny watching her hold in her laughter. My favorite was when the teacher walked behind her. I would playfully panic and point, because the nuclear bomb of spittle was about to drop. She had to excuse herself from class to explode in laughter. My charm was working.

I met her after class and asked for her number.

She gave me her business card.

I said, "A business card—who do you think you are?"

She laughed again.

We had just received our grades for an essay we wrote. To keep the conversation going, I asked her what her grade was. She said, "Um, I got an A, Mr. Man."

I responded, "I hate you. I got a C." Then I pretended to walk away mad.

She gave a chuckle that came from her diaphragm. It made me want to keep her laughing the rest of her life.

What convinced me I had a winner was when I invited her to a school dance. When the slow jam came on, she did not grind me like other girls. She kept me at arm's length, and rocked in rhythm with me slowly, the dry warmth of her hands on the back of my neck. It felt like we had been intimate, in a past life. I knew right there she was the one.

We often sat under this one particular tree and discussed life issues. Once, we got really serious talking about our goals. Hers were simple—she wanted to work in the medical field.

I told her I wanted to be a famous singer and a model. Her demeanor changed. She looked away somberly and said, "Cleon, I don't want to be associated with that. I'm a private person. I hear too many horror stories of famous men and their spouses."

I mentally changed my profession to UPS driver that day.

Eva rarely believes my stories, until someone else confirms them, or she witnesses for herself. She saw it all that day on the catwalk of the Woman's Forum. I walked off the stage and left Adai trying to quell the firestorm I created.

Backstage, all of the models stopped what they were doing and just stared at me. I did my best to keep my humble face on. After a long silence one model said, "Yeah, I guess you got that athlete thing going on." I accepted it as a compliment.

The event coordinator reminded me I still had to do a workout upstairs for a breakout session. There was a room with my name and picture on the door. When I walked in the room, it was packed with women ready to experience CJ's brand of workout.

My wife immediately assumed the role of a personal assistant, and clients of mine protected me like they were security. It was difficult getting to my room because people were pulling on me. Two of my group members started moving people out of the way to clear a path. The *Law of Attraction* was clearly in effect.

One long-time client I affectionately called "Spicy Ginger" loved my relationship with my wife. Whenever a woman got too close to me with the wrong intentions, Spicy Ginger would wedge herself in between as if she were my bodyguard. She was my "marriage-guard."

That day was one of my top five moments in life. I just knew some major talk show host or media personality was in the building and would hear about this phenomenon, snatch me up, and whisk me away from the pit of the middle class. The high was quickly over when that did not happen, but business continued to pick up and my brand was on the map. I may not have gotten on *Oprah,* but the Radio Free station gave me a small segment during their morning broadcast, called *Summer Fitness Tips with Adai and CJ.* Every day of the summer, listeners of the station would get live fitness tips from the hottest trainer in L.A.

That event did bring me yet another client, the head sales director for the station. Beyond that, the phone did not ring with any media giants. It caused me to go through a major withdrawal, like a drug addict whose high wore off.

I learned it takes more than a gift and a pretty face—getting discovered is a ruthless process. I think when you hear an actor or actress tell you they were just waiting tables when they were discovered by a big-time producer, it is hogwash. Success takes work. Sometimes it is a grind you can be proud of, and sometimes people will do the unthinkable. In the wake of social media, it is even harder. If you don't have a big following, people with influence won't even look your way.

Branded in 60 Seconds
. . . Credit a Python

In the initial planning stages of my next Fitness Syndicate vs. Obesity program, I had absolutely no room for any more clients, let alone MMA fighters. Fighters are difficult to take on because payment does not always come in cash. Most of the time it pays off in wins, with your logo attached to their fight gear or banner. When a fighter wins, everyone wants to know who had a hand in training him or her. Simply put, if your fighter is not in a premier MMA event, there is no need to worry about cash payment. Some are worth sticking with, others just disappear from lack of discipline. I became good at turning those guys down, but one in particular refused to accept no for an answer.

> In 2006, I began training for my first submission match, the highest-level event I had competed in. I trained with the number one and number two grapplers in the world. Every sparring match was a near trip to the hospital and I loved every minute of it. I was in a circle that none of the guys at work could—or would—touch. When I could not spar with these two, I traveled to other gyms I was familiar with.
>
> I had spent a little time with a man named Coach Ahmad, so I knew he had some talent to work with. One day in particular, I sparred against a man by the name of LaTeef "Python" Williams. While we grappled, I noticed we cancelled each other out. We were at the same level.
>
> It was funny rolling with him because he was always talking. He was having a pleasant conversation with everyone in the gym, while we were grappling. I said to myself, "This is one free-spirited cat."
>
> When it was over, I sparred with a few more guys and left. Just another day of training, but LaTeef was different. The night before my big grappling match, my mother passed away, so I

never got a chance to put my skills on display. So much for that—but the training I received was immeasurable.

Years later, while working out at my gym, I received a call. I heard a voice say, "Ay, CJ, What's up man. It's LaTeef."

Before we got down to business, he softened me up with conversation about all the same people we knew in the fight game. We talked about controversial bouts and training horror stories. I guess you could say I was high on conversation. Then the real reason for the call came.

He said, "So I got a fight coming up and I really need some training. Maybe you can sponsor me by helping with my conditioning. I heard you are the man."

I did everything I could to refer him to other trainers. For a while it worked, but LaTeef kept calling. After a couple of weeks, LaTeef drove right up to my gym door, came in and said, "What's up man? When are we gonna get at it?"

I shook my head, chuckled and said, "All right man, we'll work it out." I was nervous because part of me wanted to see if I still had it. But since he was not paying me, I decided to throw myself into the workouts.

I was shocked I still had my wind. I could still train endlessly. LaTeef was the same beast and matched my intensity. I threw everything I had at him: running, plyometrics, agility drills, kettle bells, tire tosses and more. No matter how tired he got, there was always a joke or a fake British accent in his griping. I needed to know how he stayed so positive.

During one workout, he told me that he was a victim of a shooting and nearly died. Doctors were baffled that he survived. It gave him a new perspective on life. He did the impossible and fought his way back to health, to a point where he was able to grapple again and seek employment in law enforcement. Now I understood his positive outlook. I understood his perseverance and lack of fear.

When we were finished training he was in the best shape I'd ever seen him. I was excited, and he was blissful, cool as a cucumber. (It should have been the other way around.)

Fight night came, and I had a front row seat to the cage. All of the fights were exciting, but I was eager for my fighter, LaTeef.

His opponent walked into the ring, standing at six feet five inches tall, with freakishly long limbs. He was pumping himself up in the ring to a point where I was nervous, wondering how LaTeef was going to approach this match.

Then LaTeef walked to the ring. His walk was extremely casual, with an air of calm. He seemed to be looking beyond victory and already to the after party. The smile on his face was like he was at home.

Observing this and absorbing LaTeef's energy, I sat back in my chair and said to myself, *This fight will be over in short time.*

The bell rang, and the fighters met in the center of the octagon. LaTeef walked up to his opponent, picked him up, threw him on the ground, and choked him out in just sixty seconds. Everyone in his camp was screaming, but LaTeef stood up, smiled, grabbed the microphone, and smoothly acknowledged his team. He was not even breathing hard.

Coach Ahmad called me into the octagon and we celebrated the victory. While inside the cage, I could see my logo hanging on a banner over the cage, along with other sponsors and fight gyms. There was no more question as to who I was: one of the best trainers in the game. To this day the banner hangs high on my gym wall.

This experience was so much better than money. It was my brand solidified. It was me losing my fears by watching a fearless human being.

LaTeef "Python" Williams did not fight again. He became a firefighter instead—law enforcement's loss.

The Fine Line Between Promotion, Giving, and Pain

The radio station hosted another major event in the fall, called *Taste of Soul*. It was a huge cultural event showcasing the best in black business, culture, food, and music. I called Rochelle and asked if I could merge another Fitness Syndicate vs. Obesity Program with the event, but this time my sister, Adai, would be heavily involved. We ran it bigger than before. This time, people who wanted to be selected would send photos, videos, or written letters to share why they deserved a fitness makeover.

The deadline for entries was the day of the event, where you had to come to my booth and hand me your letter. I had the busiest booth that day. Adai was getting really good with boxing, so we did a demonstration on a side stage. It wowed the audience. They saw her improvement and they witnessed my craft.

The following Monday we introduced the selected participants during the morning radio show. We selected the names in October, but the three-month program did not start until January. I wanted to give the participants time to get their lives in order and prepare their families for their journey. The plan was to show-case the results at the next Women's Health Forum the following April.

A local TV news station working with the radio station wanted to do a simulcast at my gym to showcase the selectees and the trainers who were helping. I was proud to have most of the trainers return from the prior year, but I was most proud that the celebrity fitness guru from the radio station, Coach E, accepted my invitation to be a part of it. New to the group were my new apprentice, Diana Redd, and Akuete Kpodar from West Africa (a truly brilliant human being who came to America homeless). I was also able to attain another celebrity fitness trainer named Dawn Strozier.

> *I met Dawn Strozier at an American Diabetes Association event in Marina del Rey. She was an ambassador and the keynote speaker, I was also invited to speak at the event. We were*

equally in awe of each other's ability to deliver motivational speeches.

She walked up to me after my segment and said, "CJ, I heard about you. You're pretty good."

I said, "Following you, I just didn't want to screw up."

We exchanged numbers and agreed that we would work together one day.

Over time, we became friends. Dawn Strozier had elevated from homeless to one of the top trainers in the game and was now a certified motivational speaker. I wasn't surprised to find she had published motivational books, but she warned me not to laugh at her photo on the book cover.

When I saw it I teased her, because she had a wig on in the photo. I said, "Is this your motivational wig?"

We both had a good laugh. I'm glad we connected.

Whenever Adai and I collaborated on television or the airwaves, there was a natural, effortless flow. Our news segment promoting *Taste of Soul* was a smash hit. It was funny and entertaining, but the message of community wellness was sent loud and clear. What meant the most to me was being able to showcase the trainers who volunteered their time for this. I wanted to give them exposure, too.

Coincidentally, my brother was in the news station that day. He was being interviewed live before my segment. The station was showcasing his work in downtown skid row. My police chief was also being interviewed about crime trends on the same telecast. I hoped he caught a glimpse of my segment. I felt very positive about the chief and wanted my brother and me to make him proud.

The Joseph boys were at it again. We always seemed to be in the limelight at the same time.

My brother's achievements drew attention on a national scale, while I enjoyed local media publicity for my work as well.

I feel a team collaboration coming someday, but until then, my brother and me have individual missions to accomplish.

After the segments for *Taste of Soul*, media colleagues, clients, friends and family expressed how proud they were. I realized when God removed me from the training unit, he put me in departments that would not feel threatened by me. Outside of the training unit, I received nothing but support for my accomplishments. I regained pride in my job as a police officer.

The news station (KTLA Channel 5) promised to follow up, as the Woman's Forum approached, and they were true to their word. The newscaster told me they did not want to play old reels from last year. They wanted my team of trainers and participants to sell it.

New for the event, the radio station wanted to add a room where men could gather. It was called "The Man Cave." I came up with a skit for the duration of the broadcast. It was the men versus the women, and it was received well by viewers.

The stage was set for another successful Women's Forum. A big reveal of the dramatic weight loss of all the participants was planned. This time, instead of male models walking down the catwalk, it would be the participants strutting their stuff and giving their testimony. There weren't any screaming women clawing at the stage. It was a mass of women and men gathered in celebration of lives changed through wellness—a more meaningful display.

I rented out a comedy club to celebrate later that evening. I wanted participants to laugh with their families and share their experiences, all on my dime. They deserved it. But when I received a call, it was difficult to fully enjoy the moment.

My brothers told me my dad had suffered a heart attack and was in the hospital. They had waited until after the women's forum was over to call, because they knew how important the event was to me. I loved them for that and I'm glad they did.

Dad was stabilized, so after the forum, I rushed to the hospital. While there, the doctor told us they could not perform surgery on him because 75% of his heart was not working. He was not strong enough, due to multiple heart attacks he'd had before. My father was dying and there was nothing we could do about it. We didn't know how long we would have him.

Previously, my brother Deon had taken my father in for two years, until Dad began showing signs of dementia. We ended up putting him in a senior citizens home for about a year, but once he had the heart attack, none of us wanted him to pass in an old folk's home. I decided that if my father made it through, it was my turn to take him in. My mother had died in a hospital and I was adamant I would not let that happen to my dad.

It soon became apparent that death was imminent, so I made up my mind to take Dad home with me, so he could pass while among family. Once I told my brothers what I wanted to do, they urged me to go back to the comedy club and finish my closing ceremony.

I tried my best to keep a smile on my face. I was sitting at the bar when Coach E noticed I was not my usual self. I told him quietly what had happened. I did not want to dampen the moment.

Coach said he knew of my father, and that I was just like him. Coach E referred to me as a "two-percenter." He explained to me that I was one of those rare people who were able to consistently bring forth ideas and make them become reality. He said only two percent of the population are capable of this. Coming from the guru himself, I was humbled.

He then thanked me for adding him to the team, but I was the thankful one. However, I was not able to revel in the glory of our accomplishment. I only had a few days until I had to bring my ultimate mentor home with me.

A week later, the local news station followed up to reveal the weight loss of the participants in our program. It was the perfect way to close the event, but it was overshadowed by the health of my dad. I could not fully taste the sweetness of completion. Things were about to change drastically, for better and for worse.

From Cynical to Singing It from the Stage

While dealing with my dad's stay at the hospital, I still had to work and run a business. Adai Lamar called me and told me she referred me to another radio personality named Tammi Mac. Tammi, along with her co-star (and my future client) Don, hosted a show that was gaining momentum. It reminded me of the radio/urban version of pop gossip and aired in the mid-afternoon.

In the show's beginning stages it was tough to follow, but that is to be expected with a developing program hosting two personalities working together for the first time. In a few months, the team found their flow and began to really jibe together.

I had met Tammi once before while producing another commercial. I was in a waiting room and she was taking a break.

She said, "Hey CJ! So, you are the trainer guy."

I smiled and said, "Yes, ma'am."

She started smacking her gum and said, "Yeah, I ain't got time for no workout, and I ain't giving up my Snickers and M&M's for anybody."

I can only describe her comment as "seriously joking." I chuckled and gave my running line, "Well, always here when you are ready."

Her energy was raw and very heavy. When you made eye contact, you could not tell if she was looking at you or through you. When she left the room, it felt like an incomplete sentence.

Rochelle, my sales lady, walked in to let me know the studio was ready to edit our promos. She said Tammi had been doing voice-overs for a lot of my commercials.

I said, "So that's the lady who brings my commercials to life. Interesting."

Sure enough, Tammi called and set an appointment. During our meeting, she seemed very withdrawn. It seemed she had something heavy on her mind. We began discussing her fitness goals and nutrition—then things went south fast.

The second I mentioned giving up sweets, she said, "I ain't giving up Snickers bars. I love my sugar."

I attempted to negotiate a plan to slowly cut down on sweets. I said, "What if we go from a full bar to a half bar?"

She began crying. It could not have been just about the candy.

Her consultation was the longest to date. She forced me to pull out every tactic possible to come to an agreement on some behavioral change. I thought I had lost a client, so I attempted to end the consultation.

Then she said, "Well, when do we start."

I was emotionally exhausted. She told me she was an actress also, and then I remembered some commercials and small roles I had seen her in. I said to myself, "No wonder I was receiving all that drama."

Our initial workouts were extremely draining. The first week, she gave her take on how her training was going over the airwaves, and the picture was not positive. She cynically verbalized in public, my battle to get her off sugar. She complained about how painful it was training with me. Not that she meant harm, but her pessimistic approach made me cringe. It was a far stretch from Adai Lamar, who at least kept me a secret.

People walked up to me on the street and said, "CJ, I heard Tammi talk about you today."

I did not know how to perceive it. I could only accept what she was doing and determine to change her tune.

Within a month, she began cooperating to some degree. She had a very high metabolism, so the small changes she made showed immediately. She went from frumpy to a more solid form in a short time, and her public cynicism slowly changed. Her co-host even noticed her change and in a comedic way, countered her pessimistic perceptions on-air.

Slowly, she began acknowledging change, in the gym and on the radio. It was like she was taking her listeners (my potential clients) through her process. At least that kind of thinking comforted me. And more listeners were coming in to the gym, so maybe I looked at it wrong.

I tapped into a new group of people from her public play-by-play. I was getting more people who were stuck in pre-contemplation. These were new clients who would never consider a ten-minute walk, let alone a trainer. I started to understand the brilliance of it. The fact was, if I failed, she would tell it with no gauge.

When Tammi started talking about small, realistic changes in her health and nutrition, her followers listened. When we crossed the threshold of improvement, we began establishing a pretty good friendship. In fact, there was a very methodical, calculated, intelligent, savvy woman under all that cynicism. We debated social, political, and spiritual issues. I knew we were becoming friends, because a couple of times we had heated arguments about my other profession in law enforcement, and she still came back for training the next day. Tammi Mac brilliantly brought out the best in me.

Tammi was training for a stage play and was the star of the show. She wanted my wife and I to come see it. The play was good, and she shined the brightest of all the cast. Her timing was incredible.

When they bowed at the end of the play, she walked offstage, came right to where we were sitting, and gave us both hugs. She looked like it meant the world that we came. The invitation meant the world to us.

As training continued, I noticed she was playing gangster rap music on her headphones. It was one of the most infamous rap groups in history. Eventually, she began asking to play it in the gym over and over again. Normally, I don't allow that type of music in the gym, but she said it was for something major and she would share soon enough.

About a week later, she was reciting lines to a script she seemed to be forming in her head. Soon after, she revealed to me that she was working on a one-woman stage play, and she really needed to get in top condition.

I said, "Having a goal is the first step to rapid change. Your mind accelerates the process because there is an end to the means."

It never fails, clients with goals and due dates, whether it be a wedding, job interview, weight-loss challenge, or event, tend to succeed. These clients are easy to train because they put complete trust in you to help them reach their targets. They know it will take more than their personal motivation, so they rely on a fitness coach. They hang on to everything you tell them, and they achieve their desired result. Half the work is done as a trainer, because their mind is made up and their vision has been clearly established. The body begins the process of change with the mind first.

Tammi was becoming lean and muscular. Her abs began to show, and her legs took on the tone of a track athlete. She was even giving health tips on her show, which magnified my credibility. For a person that hated running, she began sprinting toward the end of our runs, all while reciting rap lyrics and lines in her play.

Pouring words of encouragement made her sessions fun, and it became a work-out for me to keep up. She was becoming *a beast*. She told me her play was called Bag Lady, and it was about her life. I added boxing to her training for focus.

Finally, the event was upon us, and my wife and I received front row seats to a sold-out show. The play was incredible. It was her life story about a horrible incident in her childhood that affected the way she loved others and loved herself. She also showed how she cheated death with a flip of a coin, sending a powerful message about the AIDS epidemic. It brought the audience to tears.

From my field of expertise, the most satisfying part of the play came when she stood on stage in a bra and panties. Her body was amazing.

After the show, I looked through the program. In the "Special Thanks" portion, I saw my company name, CJ's Functional Fitness.

Tammi Mac earned three NAACP awards for her production. A major non-profit recently teamed up with her, taking her play national. My wife and I were listed as co-producers for the national stage play.

As Tammi trained, we continued to impart our life lessons with one another. She was one of my most challenging clients. The risk she took in executing her dreams gave me the strength to do the same for mine.

If you are not willing to accept challenging clients, you are not ready to grow. There are those few who know you are good, but still need to prod you to get the best from you. If you get results for this type of client, you can handle anyone.

Every week I trained her, my career was publicly on the line. I did not have to feel that way. I was already established, but if you are truly passionate about your craft, you have to humble yourself and allow your brand to be tested.

A Chance to Make It Right

The day I brought my dad home from the hospital, I didn't tell him where he was going. Because we already had a full house, and the only place we could have him stay was the upstairs office, I had to beg my wife to allow it. There was no time or need to remodel our home, given the doctor's diagnosis. I had gotten a stairlift, revamped the office and turned it into his room, all while still working my job and my business. I don't know how I did it.

When we arrived, Dad said, "Oh, we are stopping at your place?"

I said, "No Dad, you are home. Let's go check out your room."

I put him on the stairlift and got him upstairs. I walked him into his room and he cried immediately. That was the second time I had ever seen him cry. Years before, my insensitivity would not acknowledge his tears.

These were born of utter relief that he would not die in an old folk's home. He looked at me and said, "Thank you, son!"

I replied, "No, thank you, Dad. For everything."

The first night was my first test with my father living with us. I gave him a bath. My wife, doing her best to be supportive, made a great dinner. My oldest educated herself on how to help administer medicine. I had a client to train, so after Dad was clean and fed I left, telling my wife I would be back in one hour.

I told my dad I was leaving, and he said, "Go ahead, I understand. You have a business to run. You are just like your daddy."

I was in the middle of training Tammi Mac when I received a call from my wife. She begged me to come home, but would not tell me why. I rushed home.

When I walked in the door, I heard my dad crying like a child because he thought he was in trouble. He kept saying, "I'm so sorry, I'm so sorry! You don't have to let me stay here!"

As I ran up the stairs, I noticed my wife looked traumatized. She would not say anything.

My daughter Cheyanne calmly said, "Dad, he is okay. Just check on him."

I continued up the stairs and hit the smell of pungent feces. I got to the hallway and saw my dad on the floor between his room and the bathroom. Unable to make it in time, he had fallen and relieved himself on the floor. He was completely disgusted with himself and worried what my reaction would be.

I paused and just stared at him. In my mind I went back to the time when I left him on the floor crying, begging for alcohol to relieve his pain in his darkest moment.

I took a deep breath, gathered my emotions, and smiled. This was my second chance to make it right.

He said, "Son, I'm sorry. I tried. I really tried."

I looked at him like he was a newborn baby, smiled and said, "Sh--, happens."

He looked at me, wiped his tears, and let out the biggest laugh. I wanted to restore his manhood in that moment, and it worked. I cleaned up the mess while telling him how much I loved him. I gave him another bath and put fresh pajamas on him before helping him back in bed.

Then I gave my daughter a huge hug and thanked her. She had started to clean before I got home, but Eva would not allow it, and rightfully so. This was not their cross to bear, it was mine. I think my wife expected me to be upset with her, but I wasn't. I knew this was extremely difficult to deal with.

I stayed up with my dad until he fell asleep. It was 1 a.m. and I had to be back at work by 5 a.m. My older brother Troy, and my sister-in-law Tonette, arranged for a nurse to stay with Dad during the week. She was a supervisor at a senior citizens center in Long Beach and was connected to some great resources that were helpful. On weeknights and weekends, I was on my own. Cheyanne did a great job of staying on top of his meds and Zaire, early on, played games with him to keep him entertained.

I was grateful to my clients, who were understanding at the time, because sometimes I had to leave the gym to tend to my dad. Thankfully, my gym was a few blocks away from home. But no matter what was going on at home, I could not keep up and maintain my training commitments. I passed some clients to other trainers, others I convinced to join my group classes, and there were some who were sympathetic but stopped training.

I was between a rock and a hard place because I could not take sick leave from the police department. If I did, I could not run my business—that is a condition of having an off-duty permit from your job. Plus, I had a monthly lease I had to pay, so I had to make it work.

The honeymoon stage with my father was short-lived. He was regressing to a child-like state. He kept us up all night talking to himself and blasting the television at high levels. He also had a habit of sleepwalking, so he was a fall risk.

I added more cameras in the house to monitor him while I worked. I rarely slept from worry that he would fall.

He called relatives, dead or alive, in the middle of the night, complaining that he was not able to have seconds or thirds of meals. Sometimes, he made up rap songs about life in the country. The worst part was his love of smut talk shows, turning the volume up as loud as it could go. I couldn't help remembering that he wouldn't let us watch that crap when we were kids.

Sometimes, he told my brothers we weren't feeding him. I was angry when my brothers called to inquire, particularly my oldest brother, who was constantly at odds with my dad. When Dad called one of my uncles, he showed up with a box of soul food, only to find him in his room eating.

Dad would playfully wait until I walked in the room, then pretend to call Adult Protective Services. It got to a point where I was so frustrated I would dial for him. When they picked up the phone, he'd start laughing and hung up.

> *I was nine years old when I threatened to run away from home because my mother wanted me to clean up the backyard. I wanted to finish watching the cartoon Fat Albert, when my mother turned off the TV.*
>
> *I yelled, "All I wanted to do was finish the show. I'm leaving, I'm not a little kid."*
>
> *My dad opened the door and said, "Take you're a** on then!"*
>
> *I went two blocks before realizing I had nowhere to go.*
>
> *My next-door neighbor, Betty, who was an old southern racist but loved our family, laughed at me and said, "Don't you feel stupid, now take your black a** home, little Joseph."*
>
> *Not only did I have to clean the backyard, but I had a spanking waiting for me from my mother.*

My father would call me at work or at the gym, making demands. He then began accusing old business partners of coming in my house and stealing his safe. He had no safe.

I did not want to bother my twin too much for help. He had taken Dad in for two years previously. It was my turn. Deon had the slightly independent rebel side of my dad. I got the seven-year-old dependent version.

I was paying trainers to cover my classes. I had started planning my fourth Fitness Syndicate vs. Obesity program and had to maintain it because the American Heart Association wanted to partner with my program. I had also formed a partnership with Special Needs Network as the fitness ambassador for their annual 5k run.

I was a zombie. I confided in Adai Lamar, because she was taking care of her mother, who was also sick. We found laughter and relief in sharing similar stories. Other than her, I had no one else I could vent to. My wife was not handling the situation well at all, and I did not blame her. I was just grateful she gave me permission to have him come home for what was supposed to be a short time. That short time turned into two years.

God's Plan

On top of the stress I was going through, I started experiencing a chronic pain in my groin. I had been dealing with it for years, but it was growing and becoming unbearable. One day, I stood up and felt something protruding out of my lower abdominals. I discussed my symptoms with two of my clients who were doctors. Both said I might have a hernia.

I went to my doctor to follow up and it was confirmed. I needed surgery. Years of training in the academy and MMA training had caught up with me. I had to take off work for a while. Thank God I had a client who was a doctor. He set up an immediate appointment with a fellow specialist. If I had waited I would not have been able to rise to patrol supervisor at my job. The promotion was coming soon, and I did not want to be held up. When the surgeon went in, he discovered a second hernia on the other side of my abdomen. He had to patch up both sides.

Making the most of my bad situation, I recorded a social media series on what my hernia experience was like. It is still getting views to this day. But I also lost new clients and my boot camp became a skeleton crew. I was not working, and I had to take care of my dad. That was a never-ending job for me. But there was good news. I was home with him so long, we found time to be father and son.

In those moments, he poured all sorts of wisdom on me when he was in a good state of mind. In my forties, I was given the lessons I missed when I turned my back on him in my twenties. He shared what he did to help people. I'd heard the stories before, but not with such detail, some were brand new to me. His stories connected the dots, defining what success really was. When his old friends stopped by, I listened as they shared how Dad saved their homes, marriages and lives.

Some who owed him a few bucks from years before, stopped by to pay him. I knew half the reason he went broke was because he was always loaning money to people. Sometimes the money was paid back, most of the time not. Regardless, the constant theme was he was good to people. He gave them the benefit of the doubt. If you could not pay him back with money, he took payment in time and a few trust deeds.

Within a week of my surgery, I was able to gingerly move around, just in time to take Dad to the emergency room. His body was going septic because his bladder stopped working. I remember picking him up after an overnight stay in the ER. It was dark and raining hard. I could not park behind my house because coming through the garage would have been too much work, so I parked in my neighbor's driveway.

I got his wheelchair out and set it up next to the passenger side of the car. Instead of helping me get him in the wheelchair, he slid down the seat toward the ground. I caught him and pinned him against the seat, so he wouldn't slide any farther. I was not supposed to lift more than twenty pounds, let alone a two hundred fifty pound man. I was in pain, but I had no choice. I was begging him to use his legs to help me slide him on his chair, but he had no strength either.

I began crying to God, though I was angry at Him again. I was out in the rain, soaking wet, keeping my dad from hitting the ground, all while recovering from a bi-lateral hernia surgery. Finally, a sheriff's patrol car passed. It probably looked suspicious to them. I was dressed in sweats, dragging an old man out of a car.

The sheriff was kind enough to get out and help me put my dad in the chair. I am so glad it was raining hard, so he could not see my tears, a mix of gratitude, frustration, and extreme physical pain. As soon as I managed to get Dad in the front door, my wife and kids had to help me bring him upstairs—my strength was gone.

I made it back to work in time to receive my promotion but did not go to my promotional ceremony. I didn't see the point, since my dad could not be there. Before Dad's health turned dire, he attended all of my twin Deon's shining moments and awards ceremonies, of which we were all proud. I was finally promoted to a leadership position in the department, and I could not even give him that.

I had to tell Dad about all of my accomplishments while he was dying. I couldn't tell my dad publicly that my success was his.

The Show Must Go On
In the Valley

I was still recovering from my surgery and went back to work earlier than I should have. My next weight-loss program had the non-profit AHA attached to it, and I needed to get started.

We found a new daycare nurse who focused on keeping my dad as active as possible. Most importantly, the nurse was even more religious than the first one. He would sing gospel songs to my dad, read the Bible to him, and make him watch the Christian TV networks. When I stopped in to check on him, the expression on my dad's face was hilarious. He looked like a grumpy child being punished for watching bad TV. His scowl took me back to those days when mom and dad made us sit in front of the TV on Saturdays to watch corny Christian cartoons in place of the popular cartoons of the day. Our roles had reversed.

Just to jab him a little, I said, "Pop, I see you are getting the good word in?"

The glare he gave me was priceless.

I really did not care what my dad watched except for the smut talk shows. I did not want my daughters constantly exposed to them, so I did what a father had to do.

Only my core set of clients remained with me, my group classes barely held up during my absence. I needed to stay busy, so as I usually do when I'm down in the dumps, I decided to help others in need. Running my community weight-loss program was perfect. I reached out to my friends at the local radio station to promote it, but did not go all out financially, as I had before. People were familiar with the event now, so when it came around, so did the inquiries.

Most of the trainers I knew returned to assist. I know God is good, because again, no one asked for any money for their involvement. They still believed in the mission. They still saw it going somewhere, so they rode with me all the way.

I ran a commercial which included this line: "You all will be exposed to the best trainers in the fitness industry." That did not set well with one legendary trainer.

I went to my former job at Recruitment to visit old friends (now as a supervisor). Everyone was happy to see me and reminded me how proud they were of me. I was really looking for my previous boss.

All of a sudden, I heard, "Oh, so you got the best of the best, huh?" It was one of my former supervisors, Cassandra, who was now an elite trainer and had been a fitness model for years outside of law enforcement. When I was a new trainer, she'd given me pointers and I looked up to her.

Physically the best way I could describe her is "Amazon Queen." She was tall with perfect genetics, and she knew it. Like me, she had a strong brand.

She'd brought me on as co-captain for our department weight-loss challenge, which we won two years in a row. I blushed and tried to get a word in edgewise, but she was a strong-willed woman and it is always smart to let a strong-willed woman finish her thoughts.

The one-sided conversation continued into an elevator. When she finished, I explained that I wanted to reach out to her the year before, but her mother was dying. I told her she was always on top of my list, but I did not want to bother her then. I asked her if she would join my team this year. She playfully declined—then accepted.

I assembled the best team yet, then took time to select the most heart-felt participants. I was grateful that with me in recovery, and my father at home, I had a major non-profit which had its own media connection, so I did not have to work as hard on that end.

This particular challenge was special, because everyone I selected was dealing with issues similar to mine. I even chose a contestant who was involved in a non-profit program for parents struggling with autistic children. This time, I had no desire for fame and glory. I just wanted to help people because I had no help for myself.

One participant, named Sandra, had lost her son to suicide. She was ready to give up on life, had she not been selected. Some of my previous contestants donated their time to keep the new ones motivated. I allowed prior contestants who stayed in shape, to train with the new group for free. It was an all-out help-fest.

> *Ironically, whenever I'm going through a tough patch in life, I take my mind off things by helping others. It provides a sense of purpose. Plus, you end up realizing that sometimes there are others who have it far worse than you.*
>
> *As I said earlier, my brother Deon is acclaimed as one of the nation's top police officers for his work with the homeless. What makes him special should be everyone's response—treat others as equals. But it isn't.*
>
> *He treats our homeless population like human beings. He is a police officer who maintains compassion in his daily life. He serves the homeless as he would serve anyone.*
>
> *When time freed up, Deon invited me to help with a women's empowerment program he developed, called "Ladies Night." Deon educated the women of skid row on laws which protect them, while I taught them practical self-defense techniques to help them survive an assault.*
>
> *The first event was held in a fairly nice venue. It was clean, and everything was organized. But it was the second invitation that showed me the magnitude of his caring.*

The second location was a single-room-occupancy living quarters for battered and homeless women. It was like a halfway house or temporary shelter. When I walked in, it looked like a scene from a zombie movie. The place was grimy, filled with women who had not showered for days. Roaches and rodents crawled everywhere. I glanced at my brother's supervisor, who looked like he was ready to run out of there. My brother was calm and even comfortable.

Homeless people were not strangers to us. My mother and father restored many homeless lives. It had been a while since I stood in something like this, but it did not take me long to remember and relax.

As I began demonstrating how to throw a proper elbow strike, I observed this large woman rocking and staring at me like she wanted to kill me. Every move I made, she smacked her gums in disapproval. She was a fairly large woman who looked like she had been in a few fights and won them all. Another homeless woman, who was an activist, interrupted Deon and me a few times with her legal expertise. When the program was over I could not wait to leave, and I did, in a hurry.

A week later, back in uniform, walking to the local coffee shop downtown, I heard, "Hey, Joseph!" I turned around and saw the large woman from the presentation. She still had that angry disposition and was making a beeline straight to me.

I said, "Lady, you must mean my brother, Deon?"

She replied, "Naw, it's you. You are the little skinny one."

My twin was into weightlifting and was 260 pounds of muscle. I lost weight (30 pounds) in order to better train in MMA and was 197 pounds soaking wet.

She continued, "You were the one who showed them 'bows (elbows)."

I nervously acknowledged.

She got real close to my personal space, with the meanest look on her face, and said, "I had to use that a few days ago. Thank you. Boom!" She then walked away.

I did not know whether to be happy or relieved, but I know God is good. All the time.

For the weight-loss event, my wife again took on the role of mother hen to sooth people after the demanding workouts. I was the hammer, Eva was the comfort. The American Heart Association (AHA) picked up on this energy and became more proactive as weeks went by. Life had meaning for me again; this time it was sustaining. I was watching people go out of their way to support others whom they did not know. I truly did not have to work as hard on this one. I just enjoyed the show. We closed the program by announcing the results on the radio station with Adai Lamar. There was no major fanfare, just an interview with some of the winners.

Our celebration was at a Jamaican restaurant. We kept it simple. It was the most meaningful one yet. I was given an award for my efforts by the American Heart Association, which I humbly accepted. I was told that the participants were trying to write a letter to Oprah to express how CJ and crew changed their lives, hoping to elevate me to the national status I desired. Sandra, one of the participants, told me she stopped them from doing it because she had another idea in mind.

Maybe a Failure for Hollywood, Victory for God's Will

What was so good about the Fitness Syndicate vs. Obesity project, at least in my thought process, was the program was not a non-profit. If I were to run it that way, the participants could not return to me or the other trainers for future business relationships. I loved the fact that the participants patronized the other trainers after the program. I hoped they would, because the trainers had donated their time.

I did establish a non-profit called CJ's Functional Fitness Foundation, but I had no board of directors and I wanted to fully understand non-profits before I dove in. An attorney friend and mentor, who had her own non-profit, gave me sound advice against starting a non-profit without directors.

After completing the program, Sandra and a few others continued to train in my boot camps. One evening after class, she told me she wanted to sit down and talk with my wife and me about turning our program into a reality weight-loss show. She told us about the letter the group was writing and how she stopped them from doing it. I pretended that it didn't bother me, but it did.

Usually, this is how you hear about people climbing to success. There are countless stories of groups reaching out to a celebrity to bring a valued person into the limelight. I asked myself, "Why would she stop them from doing that?"

Sandra then revealed that she worked in the entertainment industry. She had a connection whom she felt would have a better chance of bringing my work to the public. She then said I reminded her of her son (an actor) who unfortunately, committed suicide. She felt I had his potential and promise. I was humbled by that, so something told me to go with her thought process. She had us speak to a woman I'll refer to as "Lady T."

Lady T was a producer who worked primarily in the hip-hop industry and had some success in pitching show concepts to networks. She even educated us on what she learned from having one of her projects stolen. When I told her what I had done with my program, she saw its potential and wanted to meet about making it a pilot. She advised she would sign a non-disclosure agreement (NDA) at the meeting before beginning discussion at the feel-out meeting.

At the meeting, I had expected only Lady T, but she brought a friend. This gentleman had not signed the NDA. I did not feel comfortable talking about my idea, especially after the advice she herself gave about the importance of NDAs. Eva and Sandra were also there, but they were invested in this concept like I was. After being duped a couple of times, I was smart enough to hold my idea.

Instead, I showed them all of my media appearances and videos. It worked. I may not have pitched an idea, but I pitched myself. Both Lady T and her friend felt I had what it took to carry a show, even hosting shows outside of fitness. Lady T agreed to meet again, just the two of us.

When I had asked Dawn Strozier to join my fitness program, I took her out to lunch with my wife. She too had ideas she wanted us to collaborate on, including speaking engagements and a book project. One of the first things she told me was she hated the name of the program. It was not catchy to her. During our lunch, I threw out a new name, "Battle of the Bulge: Los Angeles (BOBLA)." We all loved it, so I had decided the next time I ran a program, that was the name I'd go with.

I was proud that I held my cards at the meeting with Lady T, and my wife was proud of me, too. I was getting better at reading people's intentions and not being over-anxious to spill all the beans. I think the fact that I showed restraint enticed her to want to know more, and it appeared she took me seriously.

Our next meeting was in her favorite restaurant, near where Lady T lived in the Valley. She came alone, so I could be more open. Before the meeting, Sandra told me to have a treatment of the BOBLA concept ready. I researched how to make one and presented it.

Lady T was impressed with the treatment. She said, "Business people in the entertainment industry drag their feet, even when they have good ideas. It's refreshing to see someone so focused on a task."

I told her, "I hit the ground running. I have no time for games."

Lady T then asked if she could work with me to help produce the show's trailers, so we could begin pitching to networks. She offered a monthly fee to help put it together, including her connections to a complete film crew. Her monthly fee was way out of my meager budget. She knew it by the look on my face.

I threw out a counter-offer I could live with, which she accepted. I had learned my lesson from the publicist years ago.

I must say, she was impressive. She even told me to hire an entertainment attorney as we got deeper into the project. I called my friend.

> *I met attorney, Areva Martin, through Adai Lamar. She was also a news analyst and frequent consultant on many of the daytime talk shows. She had asked me to help with a major event she was working on under her non-profit, the Special Needs Network (SNN). It is an organization that helps children with autism.*
>
> *She also developed an annual event called South L.A. Gets Fit. The program gave parents of autistic children a chance to exercise for free in preparation for a 5K run at the end of the training. It was an outlet for parents who desperately needed a break from the demands of caring for an autistic child.*

> *I volunteered to be the fitness ambassador, along with a running coach in her early sixties who had the physique of a twenty-year-old. Her name was Coach Antonia Routt. Each year, I got called to do a local news segment to help promote her event. She even invited me to the charity galas she hosted, including the who's-who in politics and entertainment. I learned so much from watching her work and promote these events. She showed me there is no magic. You have to grind if you want to make things happen for yourself.*

Areva referred me to an entertainment attorney named Jamice Oxely. Jamice wasted no time when it came to discussing what she does. I wanted her to come to my next meeting with Lady T, and she did. We met in Century City, and Sandra came along. She was my co-producer and demanded to be an investor to help offset the cost of production.

The meeting was progressive. I was proud of the optic: a table of successful black people meeting to help change the world. I had to absorb that moment.

Jamice went right into it on the legalities of our venture, to a point where Lady T felt a bit taken aback.

I said to myself, "I think I have my attorney."

Jamice was all about her client interest, and that was me. She went right to work with copyrights, updated NDAs, and trademarks. It cost me dearly, but I would not risk anything with this project, having been taken one too many times in the past. I felt like a boss, the center of all that was working around me.

One of my father's mantras was, "I pay the cost to be the boss." I totally understood it now.

It was time for our final meeting with my production crew. I liked the idea of meeting at restaurants, because good food brings about good vibes.

Lady T brought her partner "Tia," who was also on the production team. Tia had much more experience in show production but deferred to Lady T's leadership on this project. I brought my wife, Sandra, Tiffany (a trusted client and volunteer assistant of mine), and my attorney. We hashed out the concept of the trailer production and set a date. It was impressive to see all these directors and cameramen who had worked on other popular shows all believing in my concept. Now all we needed was talent.

I called all the trainers who were involved in the events I'd worked, and once again, took them to dinner at the Cuban restaurant. I told them all that I was turning our program into a reality television show. Everyone was excited and quickly committed to the project. Adai Lamar agreed to act as a host. I called Jesse Campbell to be my celebrity participant, since every reality show needs a celebrity, and he accepted. Big Zoe did as well. I knew Zoe would bring flavor to the show. I also called on clients to fill in as contestants. It was humbling for so many people to help me with this project.

My goal was to highlight not just the participants' lives, but the trainers' lives also. What was going to make my fitness reality show different than others, was an authentic look at all sides of the experience. The participants felt good about it. I also called and emailed former contestants to see if they wanted to relive their experience and share their story on the pilot.

One of the trainers backed out, and with good reason. He was once at the center of a reality show that turned into a calamity and did not leave him in a good light. He knew I had good intentions, but he also knew how Hollywood works once they get their hands on something. I assured him I had complete control of the show, but I did not want to pressure him. When someone says no, accept it and respect it.

I understood where he was coming from, because in the initial stages, my own production team suggested we bring out controversy, conflict and drama, like all the other shows, to sell it. I refused. It was time for a feel-good, redemptive show.

My first taste of "the business" was when Lady T came to my home and wanted to discuss our agreement as we proceeded with the project. Her contract stipulated that she had 100 percent ownership of the show, dropping me down to talent, with the option of producer credits if their production company chose.

I don't know if I was angry that a poor R&B boy-band in the '80s got a better deal than me (a VCR and $100) or the fact that my wife cooked her best dish for her (olive-oil-fried chicken wings with corn flour). I put on my poker face and told her, "We will sleep on it and let you know tomorrow."

Long ago, I developed a twenty-four-hour rule for myself. Whether I want to say yes or not, I give myself a day to process. I use this method when people call me to borrow money. Most of the time, in twenty-four hours, the person who is asking will have found another solution. Sometimes I'll take it to forty-eight hours, depending on the individual.

I already knew Lady T's offer was full of crap. I was insulted. After all I'd shown her, she treated me like a hungry hip-hop artist. I sent the agreement to my attorney.

Jamice called me and facetiously said, "CJ, I read the contract. I just want to know your thoughts."

I replied, "Hell, *naw!*"

Jamice wrote our counter-offer, giving me full ownership of my concept and a percentage to Lady T as co-producer, if the show got picked up. I figured if she turned down the counter, then she was never interested in the show. If she signed it, then it meant she believed in the product. She inked her name on the line.

With our counter agreement signed in my favor, the filming dates and locations were locked in for my trailer. We were set to film at a track and field, the internet radio studio where I hosted my show, a warehouse in the Valley, my gym, and my home. We also took some B-roll footage at the next Women's Health Forum, where I received incredible words of wisdom from Coach E.

> *During the Women's Health Forum, Coach E was also a headliner. I was on the main stage on one side of the convention center and he led on the other side, called the Wellness Village. When I finished, I took my wife to the Wellness Village to check on the coach. He had just stepped down from the podium after his presentation.*
>
> *He saw me and beckoned us to him. He put his hand on my shoulder and said, "Brother CJ, congratulations on your project, but you need to understand that you are a star. Your project is noble, but you are carrying so many people that you are dimming your own light. Focus on your own light. It is your time. Get where you need to be first."*
>
> *Coach E's sharp truth left my wife and I in a complete trance. I knew exactly what he meant. He was right—so right. In hindsight, I probably had way too many characters to focus on for my show, with too many story lines. It might have taken away from the message.*

I was particularly proud of our filming at the track and field. That was where I felt like an executive producer. Participants gave their all in reliving the physical torture of the previous programs. I set up a huge obstacle course everyone had to go through. There was a trainer at every station motivating the contestants through it. I could not believe all these people had come together to volunteer their time.

Per my attorney, I had to pay them all one dollar. That was a little weird, but she was my attorney and her recommendations were not to be debated. I rented a trailer for our celebrities and my wife got food for the crew and cast.

The crew and directors moved on my direction. It was a powerful feeling. Whether this succeeded or not, I had done something that no one could take away. Like my dad, I would be one step ahead of everyone, so I could fill in when needed. From the editing, the theme song, and rearranging of the script, I had educated myself on what to expect so it would go smoothly. I developed a new skill set. I was officially "CJ, Executive Producer." Little did I know that more personal trials were coming to off-set the momentum of this project.

Tragedy Does Not Care About Your Passion Project

Ironically, while filming a pilot about health and wellness, my older brother, Troy, called me. "Hey Cle, I really need to get with you. I have got to get my health back. Can you help?"

I said, "Of course, It's about time, bro!" I could hear the sense of urgency in his voice.

At 52, he was suffering from the ramifications of poorly managed type II diabetes. He had been in the hospital numerous times and had most of his toes amputated. At one point, the doctors considered removing his leg.

I was more than ready to help, but there was never a follow up. I made attempts to reach him, but he stopped answering his phone. My brother had been out of work for a while due to his illness and fell into a state of depression.

New Year's Day, while working on the show's pilot, I received a call from my twin, Deon. "Cleon, I need you to come to Troy's house, now! I can see him in his den and he won't open the door. He won't move. I don't feel good about this, man."

I got in my car and drove as fast as I could to my oldest brother's home. By the time I got there, his neighbor and childhood friend had already opened the door. I walked in to see Deon trying to communicate with Troy, but he was just mumbling. There was blood all over the floor. There was also pus and mucus around the den and on the couch. It smelled like rotting flesh. He was sitting on the couch with his hand close to a pillow. He had a T-shirt on with a picture of his wife and daughter on it.

He managed to mumble that while trying to change his bandages on his feet, he fell. He said he was fine and wanted us all to go home. I called for an ambulance. He was not in his right mind and needed help. Deon and I were police officers and knew he needed medical attention, but he also needed to be evaluated due to his state of depression. He was showing suicidal tendencies. I found out that his wife and daughter were out of town on a trip.

Because of our employment, we felt it would be easy to explain to the officer and the mental health unit staff member who arrived from Long Beach what happened, and Troy would be off to the hospital. The officer looked horrified, but swore nothing was wrong.

I said to the officer, "Brother, will you please take a look at this house? It looks like a crime scene."

The mental health worker looked just as horrified, but he agreed with the officer.

I laid out all the requirements needed to admit someone. "He is a danger to himself, he's making statements that sound like he has given up, and he is gravely ill. Guys, you know you have to take him."

Deon was also pleading with the officer to do something, so he called his supervisor. When the supervisor walked in the house he turned red, so astonished by all the blood he would not even go inside the den.

More friends of Troy's had arrived. None of us had ever seen Troy in this state. He was like my father on steroids.

> Troy was everyone's hero growing up—and everyone's bully, if you pushed the wrong buttons. He had an uncanny physical strength that was gorilla-like. Troy tossed Deon and I around like rodents to impress his girlfriends All of my cousins tried to whup him to no avail. To this day, my cousins say it was just fun making the attempt. And I've heard other stories for years.
>
> He nearly beat five men to death in college, when he played football in Minnesota. Five white males wanted to harm Troy

because of his complexion. They attempted to jump him, and I guess it did not go so well.

When we did construction, our tool van broke down and the gas station was over a hill, so my brother pushed the van uphill by himself.

When tenants were purposefully late on rent and all legal means had been exhausted by my dad, he would send Troy, and somehow the rent got paid.

My dad told a story of the last time he spanked Troy. Dad got stuck under a pool table that had fallen on him. All of sudden the pool table was thrown off. Dad looked up to see the men who had helped him, but it was Troy standing in the room by himself.

While still bleeding profusely from his limbs, my brother got up from the couch and slowly said, "Leave me alone. I'm going upstairs."

I blocked him, and we were nose-to-nose. He said to me, "Is there a problem?"

I respectfully replied, "There is no problem. We have to get you to the hospital."

He said, "I'm fine, I just need to get upstairs."

He stumbled by me, and at that moment I did not have the will to stop him. Everyone in the house was pleading with him, but he was determined to get to the stairs.

Deon now blocked Troy's path, and Troy repeated, "Leave me be." Deon let him pass.

We assumed the officers would have gotten him on the gurney long before then. Deon and I looked at each other and nodded. I told the officer that we would put him on the gurney, and the officer appeared relieved. We grabbed Troy from the stairs and the struggle began.

At near death, Troy proudly showed one more demonstration of his strength, throwing his body to the floor. Deon and I felt all of that, but we would not let him go. We picked him up as he squirmed. I could feel his strength leaving him.

With one final heave, we got Troy on the gurney. His friends pinned his legs while my brother and I controlled his arms. I looked at the bewildered officer and said, "Officer, if you give me your cuffs, I will cuff him." I managed to get one cuff on. We needed another handcuff for the other arm. I said to the sergeant, "Hey brother, I need one more cuff. Toss yours to me, please."

Deon placed the other cuff on Troy, allowing the paramedics to secure him, then we took the cuffs off.

Troy said, "I'm not crazy. I just want to be left alone."

Deon told him, "We can't, Troy. You need help."

As we were putting him in the ambulance, the officer gave me his card and smiled as if he did something for us. It was like he wanted me to call the station and thank him for helping. I just thanked him and said to myself, *I'm glad I work in L.A.—we are on another level.* I would have been suspended if I handled a call like that.

We followed the ambulance to the hospital and went into the emergency room. The doctors were having a difficult time controlling Troy, so my brother and I, once again, pinned this strong-willed man until they were able to sedate him.

When he calmed down he looked at Deon and said, "Did I ask you to help me?"

When we walked out, it took everything to hold my emotions together, but when Deon teared up, I did too. To provide some levity, I said, "Well, we can finally say we out-wrestled our brother." I got a smile from Deon as we absorbed that moment.

We followed up at the hospital later. Pastor Chaney and one of our cousins met us. We kept it light-hearted. I was grateful for that. I did not want a worry-fest. The doctor told us it was more serious than the diabetes. They found that his skull was fractured. Troy told the doctor that he fell and hit his head on the tile floor while trying to change his foot gauze. That explained the blood all over his den. He was lethargic when we got to the house because his brain was swelling.

On January 7, 2015, we were all called back to the hospital to say goodbye as they pulled the plug on Troy. Our family lion. The physical pride of the Josephs had passed.

I went home to tell Dad. He slowly sat up and said, "Will the funeral be open-casket?"

I told him Troy had requested cremation.

Dad replied, "Yes, I know. If I can't see him, I don't want to go. I'll see him soon enough." He did not outwardly cry, but Dad slumped in the bed and tears flowed for hours.

With the passing of Troy, I developed a heightened sense of urgency to get the positive message of BOBLA out. This was the perfect justification to put a show like mine on the air. Millions of people were suffering with diabetes, heart disease, high blood pressure, and obesity. I fit the message behind my brother's passing into the pilot. I also wanted to put a segment in about my father and how active he was in his youth. It was a way of honoring him. This was my moment to show my dad, so he could be proud of me, but another setback slowed progress.

The Champ Goes Down, But Rises

set up a photo shoot with all the trainers at Manhattan Beach. I also needed to get some B-roll for the trailer. One of the team members of BOBLA (and one of my toughest MMA coaches), GI Joe Charles, was the king of the pier with his own boot camp on the beach. It had a flare of its own. He had a lot of pull and was able to help us get the permit to shoot there.

> *I met Joe at a fast food chicken restaurant. It was my first year on the force. I was taking a break, getting some lunch, when this huge frame walked into the place.*
>
> *He walked up to me and said, "You look like you train."*
>
> *I said, "A little—I'm a black belt in Sanuces Ryu jiu-jitsu."*
>
> *He complimented the fact that I was an officer and training in the arts. He gave me his card and wanted me to come to his school and trade pointers.*
>
> *I looked at the business card and it was a picture of him dressed like a pharaoh. The card read, "The Ghetto-Man Joe Charles. Cage Fighter."*
>
> *I laughed and said, "I'll come check you out."*
>
> *Joe responded, "Waiting on you."*
>
> *Joe was shaped like a giant pear and weighed 270 pounds. I thought he was overweight and out of shape. "If I spar with him, he'll be tired in no time."*
>
> *I went to his school and he asked if I was ready to train. He asked if I wanted to spar with his students.*
>
> *I said, "No, I'm a black belt. I'll go with you."*

The mat cleared, and we squared off. Within thirty seconds Joe threw me on the ground, put his body weight on me and turned my arm in a way that it was not supposed to turn. I had to tap out. I could not believe what happened, so I made another attempt, but he tapped me out in twenty seconds.

I was convinced it was because I was not in my dojo. I invited him to come out to Long Beach for a rematch.

When he came down he had me and another black belt tapping out numerous times.

One of my nieces with special needs was there to watch. When we got home, my niece told my mother, "Cleon got his butt kicked by a fat man."

I had to absorb that. I became his student and he was my first MMA instructor.

The beach photo shoot was going great and Joe was in full "GI Joe" mode. We all had a good time and the energy felt perfect. We planned to do a second photo shoot in the following weeks.

Later that week, Lady T and I were working, planning on other locations to film, when I received a call from Joe's girlfriend. I was told he was in the hospital from a stroke. I immediately drove to the hospital, the same one my brother Troy passed away in.

I was directed to the ICU, where I saw Joe being lifted with a robotic harness and placed on his hospital bed.

Once again, another strong man in my life, lying in bed with paralysis in half of his body. Unlike my dad and brother, who were stricken with grief and depression, Joe looked at me, smiled and slurred, "Waiting on you."

I could not believe how bright and vibrant he was under the circumstances. He told me, with the help of his girlfriend, he had been teaching a class at another school when his body went limp and he fell through a wall. There came a point in the conversation where he stuttered so much his girlfriend had to completely take over the conversation. She told me his physical therapy would only be for a couple of months.

I was a little upset because he needed a whole lot more than that. I promised him that I'd help him recover once his therapy was over. I also told him that he was still on the team and his comeback would be inspiring.

We began training as soon as we could, twice a week. Sometimes, I came to his house, other times he came to my gym. Within a few months he showed some improvement, but he was clearly frustrated.

I asked Joe if I could film a training session for the trailer and he accepted. When I showed up at his home with the film crew, he began crying. He did not think I was going to come through for him. I wanted to film his rehab to show people that if he can find the will to fight, our viewers who share his condition can have the courage, too. It was an inspirational segment that I knew would catch the eye of a production company. I then decided to film a segment of my father. I wanted to showcase his love for fitness in his younger days, plus I thought it would be a great way to honor him. (www.bobla.tv)

With the passing of my older brother, my dad's health continued to decline, and I wanted to lift his spirits. Initially, the goal was to show him my series when it was finished, but he was getting worse, so I got his permission to film him.

The camera crew showed up for the big segment along with my brother Deon. One of the cameramen went upstairs to get acquainted with my dad. When I introduced the two, Dad looked up and started mumbling and babbling.

I panicked for a minute because I was not expecting that at all. I touched Dad's shoulder and slowed my speech to communicate what we were doing.

He stopped rambling and said, "Okay, son."

With Lady T conducting the interview, my brother and I were able to tell our father how much he had meant to us. I was not sure if he was strong enough to speak, so I figured we'd speak for him.

He chuckled and nodded his head when we discussed our childhood memories of him, remembering them also. He appeared to be in the moment, and Lady T took a chance and asked if he had anything to say.

He slowly lifted his head, looked at the camera, and began sharing the brilliant life lessons he had imparted to us. He ran down all that he did in life to provide for his family and the sacrifices he had made. He made no apologies for the wrongs, because he was always doing the best he could for his family. Most important, we heard the words that every son needs to hear from his father, no matter how old they are.

He said, "I am so proud of them and I love them. All I ever did was out of love."

Everyone in the room was moved. There was not a point in the segment where someone did not become emotional. We had our footage, and now it was time to go to the editing bay.

Sadly, my father's health declined where we could no longer take care of him. My sister-in-law reminded me that she could make a spot available for him at the convalescent home where she supervised. There, he would get all the rehab he needed.

When I told my dad, he agreed it was the best thing. He said, "I thank you, son. You've done all you could. The doctor gave me a three-month diagnosis. You guys have had me for two years. I'm ready to go see your mom. There is no need to burden you guys."

Within a few months, Milton Joseph passed away, on December 19, 2015. My family was out buying a Christmas tree for the house when we received the call.

We went to the nursing home and there he was, lying peacefully. I had visited him days before, and all he talked about was going home. He told me Mom was visiting him, asking him to come home. I received a call from my friend CeCe, who told me she dreamt my mother was with my dad in spirit, and it was time.

I sat down on the bed next to the shell of my hero and called my brother to let him know.

The nurse told me that moments before his passing he was telling jokes about being with Mom and occasionally flirted with the nurses. My emotions held together well, until my brother came with his family, and then I lost it. I had to let my pent-up emotions go.

While waiting for the morgue to come, my brother and I reminded all of our children what kind of man he was. It's funny—we did not talk about his material gains, but focused on the people he helped in life. During that moment, it clicked in my head what we are really here to do in life with our influence—help others. I realized that was the true code to success.

At the funeral, people walked up to the pulpit to share how Dad helped them. When it was time to eulogize my father's life, we did not have to say much. I wanted nothing but excellence around him. I did not want a pity-party. His spirit did not deserve that.

Jesse Campbell performed. Pastor Chaney gave a sermon about the noble Bible character, Joseph. The sermon was called "The Power of a Good Name."

How fitting for the Josephs. The highlight was when we played Dad's segment from the BOBLA pilot. It brought the house to tears. We then laid him to rest for eternity with Mom and Troy. In my quiet moments, or moments of doubt, I play the video of my dad to motivate me through new platforms.

All Ready to Go, On the Shelf for Now

After all I had gone through, the trailer for BOBLA was finally finished. I even went to the editor and stretched out three episodes from all the footage. I had to take matters into my own hands.

My wife and I took Lady T and Tia out for dinner to thank them for all the work they did on the production. I also wanted to discuss how we would move forward, pitching the trailer to networks.

The dinner felt awkward. They both appeared to be on the defensive the entire time. When I asked what the next phase was, they were extremely reserved. They were frustrated with my attorney. They said they wanted her out of the picture and I no longer needed her. Both told us there was nothing more to say until we gave them exclusive rights to pitch our show to a network.

I did not understand the defensiveness. That was not the plan of the dinner.

Against their wishes, I kept my attorney and we agreed to a six-month contract. While they worked on their end, I was to build my social media. I did my part, but for six months they did nothing. That was the most frustrating part of the project—waiting for updates and receiving none. My once-a-week calls to Lady T were considered micromanaging. I had to remind her that the contract stipulated that she was to let me know whenever she made a new contact. Instead of frustrating myself more, I waited it out and when the contract expired I took matters into my own hands.

I received a call from Sandra, who was taking a production class at a university. She wanted me to come to the class and sit in as she completed her final exam. For the test, she was to present her own trailer and pitch it to the class. The instructor, well known in the entertainment business, invited a guest to the class. He was the biggest producer of one of the hottest fitness reality shows.

Some students were hesitant to present because they felt they had a good idea and did not want the idea stolen. I looked at the instructor and it appeared he was taking notes of the pitches he liked. He appeared to be a little too focused.

One student said that she won a large settlement after her idea was stolen. After hearing that, Sandra, pitched her trailer. It was very heartfelt and honored her son's life.

When she was done, there was time left, so she looked to me and asked if I wanted to pitch. With two major players in the classroom I said to her, "I don't want them taking my idea. They need to sign an NDA like everyone else. I'll pass."

Looking back, I truly believe Sandra set me up for an opportunity that I should have jumped on. I was so paranoid. I became overprotective with my product. That was the moment to strike, and I missed it, horribly.

Months later, I was able to find a new group of people to work with and pitched the show to a production company a fitness participant named Kim, worked for. They were interested but wanted to make sure I had a financial backer for the project. The one person I had to help finance the project became ill and backed out. I knew then that my project was at a standstill. I had to do something to push this idea out, so I turned to what had been working for me since the beginning of my business: the Radio Free station.

When all else failed, I decided to place the trailer and the three pilot episodes on a website (www.bobla.tv) to see if running a promotion on the radio station would draw attention to the work.

I did on-air interviews with Adai Lamar and produced energetic commercials. Since most of the radio personalities were familiar with me and my product, I knew they would sell it and they did. My police union even put a blast on their weekly newspaper, letting my fellow cops know what I was embarking on. I hosted a viewing party for all my clients, friends and mentors, and received positive feedback from all but one.

Abby had been recommended by Adai to give advice for my show concept. She had some success pitching shows and was willing to help. She understood what I was going through. Abby was very sharp, but kind with her criticism. I invited her to the screening party. She sat in the back with a smile all the way through.

After all the adulations, cheers and positive feed-back, I asked he how she felt about it. Her answer was, "It was nice, but I did not get it."

That stuck with me more than the fifty-plus compliments I got that night, maybe because she was in the industry and understood how to properly push a pilot. She reminded me that in today's age of social media, millennials don't have the patience to sit through a half-hour show. They need information in small increments of time.

I believe now that I was cramming early-2000-style pitching methods into the 2016 age of social media. It became painfully clear when I released the videos. People my age were more likely to watch all three episodes, but the young audience rarely got through the first episode. The dream of my site and the videos hitting a million views became a dismal thousand at best. Abby was right, and I humbly appreciated her for that. Yet another lesson I had to absorb.

The BOBLA project was a bust. I continued to push it through social media, just for views to promote my brand. My social media pages were growing, but views on the site did not. It got to the point where I became obsessed with making it work. It was my passion project and it was consuming me to a point of depression.

I became more frustrated, thinking about all the money I spent. I knew this project would bring the success I was looking for. That is when I heard something inside me say, *What were you in it for in the first place?*

I took a deep breath and reset my mind to a more positive state. I said to myself, *I can dwell on the pain of an unsuccessful project or remind myself who helped during this project and what skills I developed.*

When I thought about how it helped people, it changed my perspective. I kept a woman from falling into the pit of depression, helped a man recover from a stroke, allowed two coaches to share how they beat cancer, restored a woman's confidence in gaining employment, and most of all, I was able to honor my father before his death.

The change of perspective allowed me to let go, put the project on ice, and make peace. I had to let God's plan unfold, allowing natural order to take its course for His good. The lessons I learned, and the skill sets I developed, set me up for something to come later.

Don't Quit Your Day Job

While licking the wounds from my television project, I thought back to the height of energy I felt in the creation process. At one point, my confidence in the show made me think it would be picked up and millions would roll in. I threatened early retirement from law enforcement. Eva expressed her frustration with my thought process—we could not live off her teacher's salary alone.

One day, I nagged her until she yelled, "If that's what you have to do to keep your sanity, then do it."

The motivational audiobooks I listened to, intensified my desire to jump ship from the 9-to-5. They told me to take a leap of faith.

I called my mentors for affirmation. I knew they would see it my way, but when I called Mr. Evans, he told me to hold on. He said my job was supporting my business in more ways than one.

I called Areva, who was on television, and the first thing she said was, "Do you know how many people you see on TV daily who are struggling to pay the bills? This industry is no joke. You are only as good as your last project." Areva also affirmed that my job was a security blanket and said to make sure I got all the pensions and benefits coming to me.

I also remembered a conversation with my dad as he neared death. To my surprise, the ultimate risk-taker urged me to stick it out on the job. Maybe he was thinking beyond me, to my ability to support my family.

The final confirmation came from a world-famous motivational speaker named Lisa. I appreciated Lisa's kind gesture to call me directly. She told me not to quit my day job, but to use that job to save money along with my earnings at the gym, until the time was right to make a move.

The call was initiated by my friend and client Adai, who was interviewing the speaker on the radio station as an in-studio guest. Ironically, as I trained

Adai, I often talked about visions of leaving my job and diving full-time into my business. Adai also bought me Lisa's book, which prompted me to rethink my exit strategy.

Once again, I had to tell my wife she was right. I had to reset my mind to find contentment at my job, and I figured out how.

Keep Your Supervisor at Work Happy, Maximize Your Time

Since I decided to hold on to my secure job as an officer, I had to reset my mind.

Law enforcement is an honorable profession and I've always given it my best, but the political and social climate against officers weighed heavily on me. With the recent law enforcement ambushes, I constantly worried that I, or someone I worked with, would be next. I had been promoted to supervisor, and now had a higher sense of responsibility for my officers.

I combated those negative feelings by diving into my work. I stayed on top of projects and met all deadlines. I got ahead of problems instead of waiting for them to fester. I took projects from my superiors to make their lives easier, and in turn, my reward was more available time to run my business.

Favoritism didn't get me that reward—when you complete your tasks early or by deadline, you don't have to worry about overtime. Being helpful to everyone at work comes back to you when you need something taken off your plate. It is the natural law of how things work in any aspect of life.

When I sensed a negative relationship brewing at work, I'd go out of my way to find common ground. That does not mean I became a pushover. It meant I was the first to recognize that we all have to focus on the mission and not the ego. The mission supersedes a problematic person. When everything else fails, fall back on your human relations policies to work things out. Never fall into the trap of someone else's anger. There is always a better way. It is hard to do at first, but when you get good at peace, you are golden.

Also, don't reinvent the wheel unless your supervisor asks you to. Get behind his or her vision and help them realize it. If you are good to the people you work for, they will be good to you when you need a day off for a special event. Simply put, when you are a hard worker there are perks. The same law of cooperation applies to people under your supervision as well.

Being frustrated will not help you. Go to your job with the mindset of being the best within your role, so when you clock out at the end of the day, all you have to think about is your passion. Leave no stone unturned before you go on vacation, so you can focus on molding your dream. Advance so your wage, along with your pension, grows. You want your retirement to be a cushion, so you can operate your dream comfortably.

When I made those adjustments, I began to enjoy coming to work again. I looked back and saw how my job and my passion were working together to encourage my growth. I saw where the two could still benefit me. Each level of leadership I rose to on the job sharpened how I ran my business.

Recently, I walked into the academy and watched the way the instructors were training cadets. One of them, Hurt Locker (now a senior instructor), who had been in the unit months before I was removed, pointed me in the direction of exercising recruits. They were using kettle bells, resistance bands, and circuit training. The instructors were not belittling the recruits anymore but encouraging them. Instead of Physical Training or P.T. Unit, it is now referred to as Lifetime Fitness.

Hurt Locker said, "We are finally doing all the stuff you attempted to bring in."

I felt a sense of pride. The mission was bigger than me. Although I'll never get the credit, I had an impact, and I'm grateful to see the benefit.

New Platforms On the Horizon

One of the most consistent pieces of advice I've received from friends, family, clients, and mentors was to write a book. I fought it for the longest time because I did not want to write from a place of pain. I wanted to write from a place of matured wisdom. I could not write this bitter and angry. I had to adhere to the spiritual and tangible assignments given to me and see them through. I had to figure out how tragedy works for us in order to share it with you. I had to win at the threshold of losing, and lose at the threshold of winning—and not be broken, in order to have the credibility to share how I navigated my valleys of success.

As soon as I began to press the keys from the positive space I'm in now, the information flowed on the page like water. When I relived the dark times, I felt the pain, but I also lived the solutions to the next valley.

Recently, I've had nightly dreams in which a force is pulling me into a different space. The dreams are uncomfortable because I love where I am right now. I struggle in my dreams because it is natural to do so, but I'll embrace and accept what is to come.

I look at success as a means to bigger valleys. The greater your influence, the more people will come to your aid to sustain you. It means you are capable of handling more, so you will attain more. I embrace it and so will you.

A Joseph Returns from the Pit . . . a Boss

Late Summer 2017

Ten years after the humiliation of being removed from my self-defense and fitness unit in my law enforcement role, I accepted the job as a supervisor in that unit.

I spent ten years in the wilderness, but I did not lay down and die. For the last year, something inside told me to get ready. I upgraded my skills with even higher fitness certifications. I always stayed in top shape, but also recommitted to my MMA training. Primarily, boxing and Brazilian jiu-jitsu (where I excelled before). I sought out new methods of learning.

While in the pit of the valley, I mastered my craft and created new valleys to conquer. I returned with more to give. I returned with the power to change—the power to help others and to impart wisdom in my business and job.

The move happened so fast that one has to believe it was by design. I got phone calls from people who heard about my work promotion and were celebrating my return. The news brought smiles and nods of approval from those who knew my journey, and it was humbling. The look of respect from those who did not know me, but heard of my legend, was reassuring.

Like the Bible character Joseph (in the Book of Genesis), some of my brothers threw me in the pit, but now I'm coming back. I offer peace and love for them. I offer leadership. They were a part of the journey that unlocked my potential. This is still not the end—it is the beginning, *reloaded*. As we say in the "hood," "*Won't HE (God) do it!*" There is plenty of room in my valley for this, too.

The Conclusion Is Not In This Book

As expressed in the beginning of this book, this work is not about what the struggle of hard work looks like at the end of a far-removed journey. It is not written from the lap of material luxury. It comes from the perspective of a person familiar with dark valleys, confidently crossing into the bigger valley of success, planned by God. I have grown and seen God's magnificence manifested. This is fresh for me, not a distant memory.

I can paint a clear picture for you.

Know that if you are experiencing a valley, you are not alone. You should also know that the next level of success creates bigger valleys. As long as we live, the valleys will never stop. Our lives are filled with the purpose of constant learning.

This book is for that entrepreneur who may have developed fear of success and failure from watching a family member or a friend fail in their own endeavors and has become paralyzed in growth.

This book is for the person who discovered that working for someone else through their quality years is entitled to more.

It is for the person who had guidance and influence from mentors but has yet to see his platform rise.

It is for the individual who experienced some success, without it carrying him over the finish line.

It is for the entrepreneur whose brand is favorable to the public, but the bank account or the lifestyle does not reflect it.

It is for the person who may feel they've let down the people who had high expectations of them.

It is for the person who has done everything by the book, with no staircase to the top in sight.

It is for the person who finds joy in helping others springboard to success but can't seem to find their own.

My message to you is this—wait—do not quit! To do that is a sin. You are robbing God of his master plan for the world. Your dream was never about you, but about Him choosing you for his work. Your climb out of the valley is coming, and sometime afterward, your next valley will come. It will not come in the timing you expect, but the spirit will let you know when it is close.

God's timing is different than yours. The fact that you cannot control people should give you relief that you cannot control the timeframe of upward movement. The puzzle pieces are aligning for that moment.

You may have to maintain your 9-to-5 while making your business plans. You may run into life tragedies that will test your will. The more you understand how to navigate the system of your workplace, business, and personal life, the easier it will be to tolerate and even learn from challenges. Embrace all you are learning while in the valley. It is making you stronger. The valley is getting you ready for the climb.

As your valleys grow, you may have to wade into a spot or move to another part of the valley to create steps somewhere else. This is the luxury of having bigger valleys. You may have to climb back down those new steps you made, because on the climb you found the key to what was holding you down. One step forward and two steps back may lead you to greater success than you could ever image on your own.

Don't give up, and soon you will see steps around you that do nothing but climb. Some steps will be escalators—people you have helped who pull you up. Sometimes you will recognize withered thorns in your steps, that once held you back. Some of those thorns will be of human form and some will be self-inflicted. You'll understand that even the most miniscule memory, unrelated circumstance, or meaningless encounter actually had everything to do with the threshold you are about to cross.

Never allow these phrases to seep in and dwell in your mind when in the valley:

- I'm too old
- I'm too young
- I'm not good enough
- I'm not educated enough
- I don't speak well enough
- He or she is better at it than me
- I don't deserve to be successful
- I have no time
- I have no energy
- Technology has passed me by
- I'm not attractive enough
- I'm not experienced enough
- I was born in the valley
- I'm not a man
- I'm not a woman
- I'm not white
- I'm not black
- My past is holding me back
- I'm trying
- I don't have enough money
- I'm not healthy
- I've hit rock bottom

Each one of these excuses has an anecdote to build your steps out of the valley.

Read aloud:

- I'm seasoned for the moment
- I have the energy to make this happen
- I am the best for the position—they just don't know it yet
- Life has taught me how to handle the task, and what I don't know I'll find out
- While learning to speak, I have people who can speak for me
- No one is better than me at being me
- I will dive in to technology—I'm capable of learning
- I am a sexy beast—it is their loss if they can't see this
- I bring something to the table no matter how much experience I have
- I recognize it is time to fight my way out of a bad situation; enough is enough
- Thank God I'm not a man—I can do it better as a woman
- Thank God I'm not a woman—I can do it better as a man
- This field can use a little pepper in its salt
- This field can use a little salt in its pepper
- My past is the key to everyone's success
- "Try" is not in my vocabulary. I will continue to do better
- I can use my health struggle to help others
- It cannot get any worse—bring it on!

If you noticed, some of my anecdotes were a little wordy. I had to put effort into processing them, but this is what I want you to understand, success is a challenging process and it takes work. The Bible records this truth in multiple places.

The 23rd Psalm tells us, "Yea, though I walk through the valley."

1 Kings 17:2–6 says while wandering in the journey, God sent ravens (resources) to sustain.

In the book of Genesis, Joseph was elevated to royalty, but if God had told Joseph what he had to go through to become royalty, would the man have embraced the vision? I think not. The vision was the ignition; the journey was the practice of faith; the next platform was the reward of expanded territory.

You will learn like I did, to look forward to the next valley, because your track record in climbing out of past ones gives you something that makes you a better navigator. Iron forges iron. Whether you come out of your valley in your youth or old age, the feeling of bliss will be the same. Your climb out may not look like the plan you envisioned. It may be different, but even sweeter.

When you close this book, take a moment to look at the TV screen or open up your laptop, then stream social media and you'll find me there (www.cleonjoseph.com). Look up on stage and see your guest motivational speaker—it will be me inspiring you on a talk show. It's me giving an online seminar on success. And it will be me live on stage, in the glow of success, reminding you to embrace the valley. It will be me on the radio. It will be me at my book signing. It will be me at the top, ready to pull you up from that last step. It will be me creating more valleys for you to climb into and out from.

I've discovered reaching success from the valley is not a material measure. It is not about acres and bank accounts. If that were the case, why are some millionaires and rock stars killing themselves due to misery and debt? If that were true, why do we hear stories of athletes and wealthy socialites drugging themselves to find bliss? They have everything, but somehow lost their life's worth. It is because they are being used up instead of being useful to people. They misused the gift God gave them to share.

I once thought that helping with my gift would get me material gain. I thought it was a barter system with God. I had to readjust my definition of success, understanding He makes successful venues where you can work. He can show you the fruits of your success with reward or He can encourage you through people you've helped.

If God needs me to live in a mansion to show people in mansions what real success is, he'll put me there. If He chooses, I'll be prepared to thrive there. Where he has me now is awesome.

Right now, my platform is evolving into a different shape, in order to save lives, inspire job creators, cure depression, counsel young minds, fix relationships, restore health, revive careers and serve my public. I must recognize the evolution timing, or God will push me in a direction where I have no choice but to transform or lose everything. I could potentially die. No matter what, He still loves me but wants to mature me.

I know this because the lesson I failed to see early on was how people sustained my father because of his influence. In his dark moments, it was people he influenced who kept him afloat. He believed in the wealth of people. People were his savings account, sustaining him until I had matured enough to bring him home with me, to finish the lesson I was meant to learn before he passed. He may not have died a millionaire, but his drive made millionaires. He may not have had the materials, but he had the influence. His valleys became huge, but so were the avenues he climbed.

God blessed me enough to have success despite my consequences, obstacles, and pitfalls. My father had an empire to leave for his family and lost it all. It was not totally his fault.

If I had helped when he needed me most, maybe I would have learned these lessons a lot sooner. I might have mastered the blueprint he set before me at a very young age, but I hid and let the ship burn.

The symbolism of life in Bible stories truly mimics life. In the Book of Exodus, Moses defied God and still was allowed to lead, and at least view the

Promised Land as his people passed through. And the people of Israel still had to *work* in the Promised Land.

In the Book of Judges, Samson was so humiliated after falling prey to his consequences that he begged to die with honor, doing God's will. He needed the strength to *push* the pillars down, destroying his enemies.

In the Book of Jonah, Jonah refused a direction of God due to comfort, and had to *rethink* his position while in the belly of a whale.

In the Book of Luke, Peter denied Christ, and Christ still gave favor to him.

I refused a proven formula and wandered in the valley until my ego was stripped away. I paid for my pride with a much longer walk in the wilderness than needed. I fell before my Maker at the bottom of the valley and acknowledged I needed his guidance. God sent pieces of my father in the form of some incredible human beings. Some to test me to see if I learned. Some to retrain me. The ones who did, taught me lessons, so my father only needed a few words to finish it before passing on.

I did not have to suffer as long as I did to find the true meaning of success—or maybe I did. Success is truly the ability to handle larger valleys, not to run from them. When you run, you pay a dear price that silently kills you. Believe me when I tell you, mediocrity for the entrepreneur is death.

These entrepreneurial platforms or valleys that I have shared with you are grooming points for the next level. My next level may not resemble what I've been blessed to do in the past, or currently. My next platform may very well create another valley. I may need more acreage to build my steps. I may need more room to attack those challenges. I may get more space to operate as I grow. Success is a continuum of forged challenges to keep you focused on the integrity of your work. You'll have it at whatever level of success you or your legacy acquires.

In my spiritual maturity, I realized that my father's plans were not God's plans for me. God put a mission in Dad's heart that worked for him. What I inherited from my father was the same drive, but a different mission for God's glory, navigating me through life's never-ending valleys. Hopefully yours, too.

Keep your eyes open on the free-fall of life's roller coaster valleys, whether it be yours or that of someone you admire. Do not focus only on the way up. The growth begins at the end of the fall. Pay it forward while you're here. Pay it forward when you're gone. Be well, Beloved.

Ezekiel 36:27–28 (KJV)

And I will put my spirit within you, and cause you to walk in my statutes, and ye shall keep my judgements and do them. And ye shall dwell in the land that I gave to your fathers, and ye shall be my people, and I will be your God.

I love you, Milton Joseph.

Prologue

Never tire of valuing people. Admiration and unprovoked loyalty are so much stronger than hanging a carrot over someone to prod them to be their best.

So many spiritual experiences have evolved through people coming together, strengthening me. As you read, I pray you will have the same happen for you. We are not alone in our need for spiritual strength.

In the 23rd Psalm of the Bible, it says, "Yea, though I walk through the valley." 1st Kings 17:2–6 tells of God sending ravens to feed the prophet Elijah while he was in hiding; sustaining him as he waited or hesitated with his next move.

What I'm conveying is that you have to do your thing while God grabs people to do His. At the crossroads of his provision and your efforts, lies his gateway to your success.

My inspiration for this work is to give you that much-needed shot of confidence in achieving the American Dream while living the day-to-day struggles or adventures of life. God uses human beings working with us in the valleys, while we pursue success. We are all entitled to what this country gives us, if we put forth the effort. I do recall some characters in the Bible celebrating before an outcome. It was an act of faith for some; for my non-faith-based believers, consider it drive.

I know many of you don't read the Bible for inspiration, and I'm not attempting to convert anyone. The Bible is simply the trigger that ignited me to write this. When you see me next, I'll be explaining it to you over the airways of radio, on the couch of a talk show, or standing on the stage of a think-tank seminar.

I now embrace the valleys, because they help me see and consider where I am going. If you want success, it is "out there." You have to climb to get it. You will become stronger internally and externally from the climb. Like me, you will be ready to accept the crossing of success, when God strengthens and promotes you into bigger valleys of success with the help of human interaction.

He also forces you to grow through the consequences of your missteps. Working together with your Maker, you will succeed, but with success comes a new valley. This cycle never ends, unless you quit.

I was inspired to write this work after helping thousands succeed in their overall health and wellness. I found that fatigue becomes truth serum for a lot of my clients. Their life problems are disclosed in the most demanding parts of my training sessions. I break them down physically, but recovery builds them up spiritually over time.

It is at the breaking point where full disclosure begins and the core of what made them unhealthy is revealed. Failure, pain, grief, abuse, and embarrassment are exorcised—it is there I am able to show how I navigated through my many valleys. I love watching their lives improve as my clients master their total wellness. I strongly believe sharing the commonality of struggles from a coaching perspective is a major part of their internal and external results.

This book is for the person walking in the valley on the way to success. I want to encourage all to embrace the challenges as they come. I want you to know your work is leading to something bigger, if you do not give up. Don't allow fear of failure (or success) to keep you from your goal.

Special Thanks

Let me thank my "In the Valley" supporters for helping me climb. Each of you has no idea how you affected my life to this point. It was your prayers, friendships, honesty, monetary blessing, excellence, boldness, mentorship, understanding, brilliance, and—most important—your love. You all have qualities of my father (no wonder I hold you in high regard). All of you are ravens that kept me sustained in my walk. You all are the building blocks of this work.

To my wife, Eva: you set the bar and continue to make me leap to my potential. I am not ashamed to say that you grew me and that I looked up to you in my youth as much as I love you today. Your dignity is your sexy and I am excited about our next chapter. Special thanks to Abdul and Evelyn Khan for giving her away to me.

To Cheyanne and Zaire: you little munchkins were the best thing that came from me. You inherited the same spiritual success—have faith in it. It is bigger than what your mom and I could provide. God has you as he has me. We are Josephs and our success lies in our helping others. The legacy is yours.

To Pastor Joseph Chaney: thank you for all of the counseling and ministry to me as a youth that led me to Christ. You are missed in the most fatherly way possible. Enjoy a well-deserved eternal bliss.

To my brother, Troy Joseph: you were my hero and always will be. You and dad walked this planet like you owned it. Thank you for showing me with your walk. Rest peacefully, big bro.

To Chaplain Mike Wise: I miss you dearly. There was a sweetness to your honesty about how God works in people. You deserve all the love from God in Heaven you have given to me and others wearing the badge.

To my brother, Deon: you are a rock star. May you continue to shine with the lion's share of spiritual gifts God gave you. God bless you and your wife, Toshi.

To my niece, Troya Joseph: you are Troy's perfection and our gain. Troy and your mom, Tonette, did a hell of a job. Thank you for letting me honor him in this platform.

To my nephews and God-children, Xavier, Deon Jr., and Jordan: I'm so glad that you have a righteous man in your father. I'm glad that all I needed to be for you is the fun Uncle, but I'll step in as needed no matter where we are in this life. That is my promise.

To my Harris nieces and nephews: it is amazing how Mom and Dad's love and strength shine in you. I am proud of you all. Time will continue to prove that.

To Pastor Wayne and Myesha Chaney: in life, there are people specifically designed by God who possess the keys to unlocking potential. Your messages did just that. Continued blessings to you both.

Mr. Charles Evans: you altered the course of my life, you rebirthed my mind, and got me to see the bigger platform. I don't just get to look at the Promised Land—I've crossed over and the work continues. I am paying it forward.

Humble thanks to Michael and Julie Bates, Steven and Barbara Warfield, Urban Showe, Gregory Allen, Deacon Dana Taylor, Anthony White, Anthony Jackson, Julian Williams, Nathan Ewert, Tom Datro, and Tim

Collins, all who were sent to lift me in times of despair and you may not have known it.

Special thanks to my adopted soul sisters and brother: Adai Lamar, Glenda Greene, Tammi Mac, Keaver Brenai, and Jesse Campbell. You all are unbelievable human beings. May our energies continue to feed from each other and grow in success.

Thanks to my prayer warriors: Celia Komathy, Li'l Sis Nancy Avelar, Yvonne Gordon, Rachel Beserra, and Sylvia Quidera. Your prayers and visions have come to fruition. God is real.

Thanks to my heartfelt supporters: Sandra Young, Tiffany Duvernay, The Miss Fits, Percy L. Tolton, Jackie Glover, Danny Matthews, Lonya Graves, Wilbur Watson, Brian and Sheila Butler, Shontae Jones, Kinji and Cherie Mack-Comegys, Ebony and Anatole Batiste, Violeta Llamas. To CJ Super Clients: Alma Moore, Elizabeth Covington, John Nyugen and wife Nela, Dreymond Jones, LaTeef "Python" Williams, Angela Simon, and former client Aurora Talavra-Phillips. Your intensity and high expectations as clients formed the blueprint for my training methods.

To my fitness family: Apollo Martin, Kelvan Gamble, Akuete Kpodar, Henry Chukwurah, Diana Redd, Natacha Nelson, Chai and Davon Brazil, Cassandra Britt-Nickerson, Jon Crosby, Dawn Strozier, Erich "Coach E" Nall, Coach Sean Waxman, Eric Washington, Coach Antonia Routt, Glenn and Jocelyn Chang, Debbie Danger, and Amy. You are the best of the best.

To my fight friends: Richard Dewberry, Burnis White II, Joe Charles, R1 Crew, Ahmad Reese, Aloisio and Moriera Brazilian jiu-jitsu and Sanuces family: the lessons I learned in the world of combative sport was spiritual and will continue to be my form of yoga when I need to clear my head.

To my media family at Radio Free 102.3 KJLH: thank you for putting CJ on the map. Thank you Rochelle Lucas, Edward Evans, Don Amiche, Kevin Nash, Nautica D., and staff for quality business relationships.

Thank you to my internet radio friends From New Day and Twilight Talk Radio: Lynette Jones and Tasha Cerda. My time in your studios prepared me for the next level.

Thank you to my entire BOBLA production team. I learned so much working with you all and watching you help put my vision together. What a ride! To all participants in my Fitness Syndicate/ BOBLA programs through the years, I've learned so much while serving you. Thank you, Abby Harris, for honest advice.

Thank you, Areva Martin and Jamice Oxely. The world just needs more power brokers like you two. You are not just role models to young women. Your excellence is a role model for all.

Thank You AHA, ADA and Special Needs Network for partnerships through the years.

Special thank you to Anne S. Hall, Suzanne and Shawn Kuhn of SuzyQ 4 You. The coaching through this process was incredible. The honesty in the discussions of this work made it so much better. Thank you, Anita Agers-Brooks for the proofing and editing of this edition.

Finally, I'd like to thank my police family. We have done some great works together and my agencies' policies, professionalism, and core values gave me the blueprint to run a business with integrity. My department continues to teach me lessons I was not able to complete in college, and it always placed me where I was needed. Whether it was advice, a book reference for growth, friendship, work ethic, showing impeccable leadership, and allowing me to study your successful traits, trusting me to lead under your guise, providing a high functioning work environment, or just standing tall for me in moments of grief and loss. You are a part of this work and I hope to continue to make you proud.

Romans 828 (KJV)

And we know that all things work together for good to them that love God, to them who are the called according to his purpose.

About The Author

CLEON (CJ) JOSEPH, CEO of CJ's Functional Fitness, is a premier fitness coach in Los Angeles, with almost thirty years of fitness and martial arts training. He has multiple fitness certifications from the National Academy of Sports Medicine. He is also a 22-year law enforcement veteran in Los Angeles, and recently accepted a role as a supervisor for his department's self-defense and fitness unit. CJ has been featured as a guest trainer on the Radio Free 102.3 FM KJLH's *Steve Harvey Morning Show* with Adai Lamar for a segment called "The Summer Fitness Minute," KTLA Channel 5 with *Gayle on the Go,* KCBS/CAL 9 for *South LA Gets Fit* and The Word Network. CJ has worked tirelessly with non-profit organizations like the Center for Lupus Care, the American Heart Association, the American Diabetes Association, and Special Needs Network to spread the message of wellness all over Southern California and beyond, along with his own community program (Battle of the Bulge LA), motivational speaking engagements, and workshops on wellness.

Learn more about the author at:
www.cjffpublishing.com

www.ingramcontent.com/pod-product-compliance
Lightning Source LLC
Chambersburg PA
CBHW071304110526
44591CB00010B/774